ROLAND BRECKWOLDT became a leading advisor on agriculture and the environment. He was made a Fellow of the University of New England and has been an Honorary Lecturer in the Fenner School for Environment and Society and a Visiting Fellow in Human Science at the Australian National University. He is the author of highly acclaimed books including *Wildlife in the Home Paddock* and *A Very Elegant Animal: the dingo*, and twice the winner of the Royal Zoological Society's Whitely Medal. He is a widely respected horseman.

THE NEW
RINGER

THE NEW
RINGER

ROLAND BRECKWOLDT

ALLEN&UNWIN
SYDNEY • MELBOURNE • AUCKLAND • LONDON

First published in 2022

Copyright © Roland Breckwoldt 2022

Allen & Unwin
83 Alexander Street
Crows Nest NSW 2065
Australia
Phone: (61 2) 8425 0100
Email: info@allenandunwin.com
Web: www.allenandunwin.com

 A catalogue record for this book is available from the National Library of Australia

ISBN 9781761067839

Map by Mika Tabata

Set in 12/18 pt Sabon by Midland Typesetters, Australia
Printed and bound in China by Hang Tai Printing Company Limited

10 9 8 7 6 5 4 3 2

For Dan and Max

CONTENTS

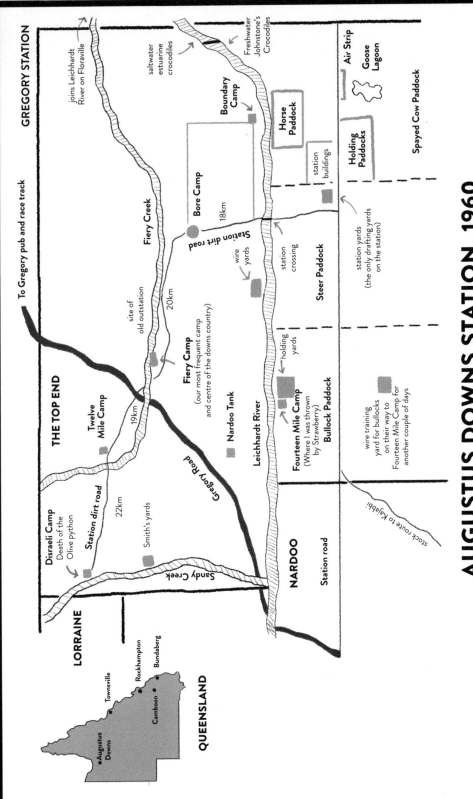

AUGUSTUS DOWNS STATION, 1960

PROLOGUE

Time measured by distances, people, incidents. I feel them in footsteps, paces, touch of foot on ground. From childhood house to bush and the creek that ran through it. From cattle-station buildings that housed our quarters to a distant cattle camp next to a beautiful waterhole where crocodiles swayed waterlilies. A dusty horse yard, ringed by rails. Then riding to the farthest point of a day's mustering. Later, on our farm, the walk from house to the dog kennel, to the chook shed, the water pump on the creek from which we pulled water.

Every feature alone. Then, the collective impact. That is what I want to write about. How land and water, the wildlife, the horses and cattle shaped me and the people I shared them with.

1

THE ARREST

Christmas Eve 1941 is my pivot, although I had not yet happened. That quiet night, right at the moment my father was lighting the candles on the Christmas tree, the military police burst through the door and arrested him. Angela watched her father being led away and him saying that 'these men are just doing their job'. Angela was three and cried herself to sleep pretending her pillow was her father. Her present of a beautiful doll's house with blue velvet carpets crafted by her father gave no comfort and was soon lost in the disruption that followed. She still feels it and there are tears in her eyes at the telling.

This is no exaggerated family legend fed by the years. While the exact time is missing, the official record confirms the arrest. Absent, of course, is any feeling. The date says enough. The Australian Military Forces Report on Prisoner of War records the 'Capture of ENEMY ALIEN N.1597 Alfred Franz Breckwoldt on 24/12/41 at Flat No. 1. Sefton Court, Frederick Street, NRTH.BONDI.'

I can now see it all.

There was always a quiet, excited anticipation on Christmas Eve for us German kids as we waited in the room next door for my father to light the candles on the Christmas tree. Our entry ticket was when he and Mum sang the German carol 'Ihr, Kinderlein, kommet'. We would rush to open presents laid out under a beautifully decorated Christmas pine tree that glistened with candles. It was always cut from a northern hemisphere pine; any pine in a park or by the roadside was in danger of losing a branch. No casuarina cut from the bush, like some Australian families did, would ever do for us. How would that look beside his beautifully crafted nativity scene, with its peaked and snow-covered stable roof?

We would get our presents early, while our friends had to wait until Christmas Day after Santa distributed his goods. Without chimneys to climb down into their fibro houses, they left a window open, with a beer and a slice of Christmas cake to lure him through. Both were missing before dawn, proof for them that Santa was real.

So why a Christmas Eve arrest? The Security Service would have known that Christmas Eve is when Germans celebrated Christmas. My father had been in Australia almost four years. They knew where he lived. He had conformed to all identity checks, such as being fingerprinted at Victoria Barracks two years earlier. How about a New Year's Day arrest? Or letting it go for a week or two until after the Christmas break? Let alone the bigger question: why arrest him at all?

My father had done his silly and misguided bit to direct enmity his way. You had to know him. He had been interviewed by two security agents on 22 December 1941, only two days before that ugly Christmas Eve. Also hovering over that interview, or perhaps even directing it, was the Japanese attack on Pearl Harbor on 7 December 1941, which brought the war to the Pacific. No longer was the war far away in Europe; it was now right here, with its waves breaking over nearby Bondi Beach.

The two security agents probed my father's allegiances and asked whether he regarded himself as a good German. There was an easy way out: all he had to say was how much he loved Australia and how much he hated Hitler. And how he had witnessed the militarisation of Nazi power in Germany and got out while he could. No need to fake that; it was all true. Instead, he insisted that being a 'good German' was a precondition for being a good Australian. He had a point, but it was not worth making. Everything was lost and the security agents fixed on the words 'good German'.

Fate, in its mysterious convolutions, had landed my parents in Australia just in time for another war. They arrived in Australia in early 1938, with only a year of freedom before Prime Minister Menzies declared war against Germany on 3 September 1939. That was soon followed by the National Security (Aliens Control) Regulations 1939 (Cth) that created 'enemy aliens' out of all migrants from countries that were now at war with Australia.

These regulations made enemy aliens out of German, Italian and Japanese, some of whom had been in Australia for many years. Worse still, Australian women married to enemy aliens lost their British nationality under the *Nationality Act*

1920 (Cth) and suddenly became enemy aliens. The regulations covered every aspect of the lives of its enemy aliens; now they were stateless and without citizenship rights. They and their families were registered with restrictions placed on employment, travel, transfer of property and ownership of cars and radios. Only English was allowed in public places and on the telephone.

My parents had left Germany in 1933 to begin a new life in Shanghai. One reason my father left Germany that year was that he had fought in the First World War and wanted no part in another. He was also an architect interested in public works that were being shelved in favour of weapons during the militarisation of Germany under Hitler.

The second reason was that he had fallen in love with the daughter of his wife's doctor, who was some nineteen years younger than him. He had left his wife, who was in and out of sanatoriums with tuberculosis; he had also left his two children, Helmut and Geisa, for the beautiful young Ilse, who would become my mother. She with the olive skin, the dark wavy hair and the clear brown eyes set in a harmoniously balanced face. My father slim, of medium height, handsome with his more angular face. Their perilous age gap tucked away.

Mum's family opposed the relationship and cut all communication. My father was not yet divorced so they departed for Shanghai, where they lived together at a time when that was not the norm, and it's surprising to hear how and when that popped up. They developed a successful architectural and interior design practice. Their brief, golden years.

There are photos. One of Mum in a white coat with her collar turned up and with a finely knitted beret tilted over neatly short brown hair. It bore the mark of a commercial photographer and has the word 'Shanghai' printed under it, and was probably a wedding photo. Another of Mum gracious in a rickshaw. My father by the sea in a shiny new convertible. Both of them in jodhpurs after a day riding.

These photos were never looked at by us together as a family, their past never discussed while they were alive. Too many skeletons. I look at them today and get teary. Regretting all those many wasted years during which I hardly knew them. They did not let me know them: their feelings, dreams, all hidden. Dangerous things. The acorn did not fall far from the oak and I would become just like them.

Angela was born in Shanghai in March 1937, just before bombs fell near their house in Bubbling Wells Road during the Japanese invasion of July 1937. There is another photo of a crowd standing around a nearby bomb crater. Ironically enough, being Caucasian, they found safety by moving to Japan. My father worked in Tokyo, restoring Japanese temples while searching for a peaceful country where he could start again. There he met Mr McFarlane, an Australian who said to him: 'They like and need people like you in Australia.'

Those few words from McFarlane changed their lives, and mine, even if I was postponed, or not yet even contemplated. This one likeable Australian with those few kind words had Holm saying to Mum 'If they are all like that then we are going to Australia.'

That is all that is known about Mr McFarlane. Was he charismatic, handsome, forceful, speaking with quiet sincerity—or all those things? A web search reveals that there was a J.N. McFarlane at the Australian Trade Commission in Tokyo at the time my father and Mum were in Japan. A phone call to the Department of Foreign Affairs and Trade gets me a machine that answers, but never replies.

When my father disembarked in Sydney, landing permission was granted to him and his wife and child by the Department of the Interior, Canberra. But Mum had stayed behind in Tokyo with three-year-old Angela to organise the transport of all the artefacts they had accumulated in China and Japan and to wind up their business. She departed Hong Kong on 30 May 1938.

I need to get something out of the way here. My father had a thing about his name; no doubt he was offended by the way Australians turned his Alfred Franz Johannes Breckwoldt into Alf, Fred or Frank. They had no right to enforce their drawling assumption of familiarity in the diminution of his grand German names. Somewhere out of his history hat he chose to call himself 'Holm' henceforth and that secured his boundary, even if 'Harry' might have been lurking.

My father actually hated being called Dad. Any inadvertent 'Dad' would have him take me by the ear and enforce, with clenched jaw and grinding tension, that I must always address him as 'Mein lieber Vater'. Before going to bed it had to be 'Gute Nacht, lieber Vater'. I never uttered either unless confronted and forced.

My younger brother, Chris, copped the same response,

6

so our father remained nameless to us during his entire life. We still refer to him as Holm as we try to work out what made him tick and how he made us tock. So, rather than refer to him as 'my father' throughout the following, he will become Holm from here on.

Following his Christmas Eve arrest, Holm was held at a First World War internment camp at Moorebank on the outskirts of Sydney. He was allowed an appeal; each state and territory had an advisory committee appointed to hear and decide the result. That appeal was held on 16–17 February 1942. The chairman was His Honour Mr Justice Pike, a retired first judge of the Land and Valuation Court, a position he had held from 1921 to 1937. Two other members were Mr A.R. Watt, a King's Counsel and leading Sydney barrister, and an untitled Mr S. McHutchison. Representing the minister for the army was Captain Hereward John Humfry Henchman—yes, that is his correct name. He was thirty-eight years of age and already making his mark as a member of the council of the New South Wales Bar Association. He later became a judge in the New South Wales criminal court.

Henchman had been appointed a captain of the Australian Army Legal Corps in 1941 when he was working on court martials. He was also the warden for the National Emergency Services in Woollahra, which protected its citizens against air raids. Only one month after the interrogation of Holm he led the investigation into the Australia First Movement, a pro-fascist group advocating independence from the British Empire and a political alliance with the Axis powers of

Germany, Italy and Japan. It was supported by prominent Australians such as Miles Franklin, Eleanor Dark and Xavier Herbert as well as *The Catholic Weekly*. There can be no doubting Captain Henchman's values and attitudes when it came to finding Nazis under Australian beds.

A minister in the Commonwealth parliament had asked, 'Why should Australian soldiers be killed at the front while Germans in Australia roam around free?' In any court of law, Holm would have known the specific charges against him and the evidence required to defend himself. Witnesses would have been cross-examined, and the judge hearing the case would have disallowed irrelevant cross-examination. Holm was without any legal representation or support; the rule of law was suspended and justified in the pursuit of national security.

Holm prepared his appeal statement with an astounding command of the English language. Where did he learn that? All the things I will never know about him. He also listed impressive referees, among them the secretary of the New South Wales Railways W.A. Newman, who had commissioned Holm as architect for The Chalet at Mount Kosciuszko, a government tourist initiative intended to promote the rail journey to Cooma. Another referee was Anthony Hordern from the department store dynasty, for whom he had under-taken architectural and design work at their Sydney store and famed rural mansion, Milton Park at Bowral, which is now a luxury hotel. There were eleven such prominent referees. Tucked among them were a Mr and Mrs McFarlane with the comment: 'Brother in law of the above, whom I consulted many times in Tokyo about conditions in Australia.'

The transcript of Holm's appeal to the advisory committee covers seventy-two A3 typed pages. I still find it unbelievably painful to read. Much of it trawls through his personal relationships and financial status. The chairman indulged in blatant voyeurism as he delved into Holm's life in Shanghai. He and Mum, who had lived together unmarried until his divorce came through, had been living in sin when it was a sin. He was questioned about the legality of his marriage to Mum and why he had left his wife and children behind in Germany. None of it was their business, but the committee enjoyed the salacity.

Then came their Sydney harbourside abode. Photographs were closely inspected of the interior Holm had designed and built for the unit they rented at Darling Point. They had been taken and published by the magazine proprietor Sydney Ure Smith, who was another of his referees. Instead of being an indication of Holm's initiative and ability to adapt, the address of this unit was treated with the suspicion that he was living by the sea to report to Germany on shipping and navy movements.

My parents' financial situation was dire, and they lived hand to mouth on what my father could earn as an interior designer. That is why they had moved to cheaper accommodation at Bondi. When they applied to the German government for sustenance support of 12/9d, administered by the neutral Swiss consul, the advisory committee regarded it as a sign of allegiance to Germany.

While in Shanghai, Holm had made a trip back to Germany on the Trans-Siberian Railway to purchase items for a major commission; he had returned with nothing. The committee had all the documentation, with the obligatory 'Heil Hitler' under the signature of his letters to Germany. Holm said that there was no alternative to signing letters without that herald if you wanted to do business in Germany, and likened it to 'God Save the King' being sung so widely in Australia. They pressed him about the business trip, believing it masked reporting information to their enemy. That was confirmed to them by Holm returning with the client's money unspent, reporting back that there was much better material in China to work with. That also led to the following interchange:

Watt: How did you come to go away from the Chinese art and seek all this adornment from Europe?

Breckwoldt: I actually intended to create a modern Chinese style in this big job. It has been done in Nanking. My competitors in Shanghai started to copy the Chinese Temples, and my opinion was different and I thought modern Chinese. I tried to create a modern Chinese, which was a cultural development in China.

Watt: Surely that is absolutely repugnant?

Breckwoldt: May I ask the meaning of repugnant?

Watt: Entirely opposite to the love of Chinese art, to decorate in modern Chinese: is that not a desecration of Chinese art?

Breckwoldt: No. The Chinese table and Chinese chair are uncomfortable and it is difficult to make a new Chinese chair in modern comfortable size and weight. It was a very interesting thing to do, this decoration.

Watt: With all respect to you I think you were debasing Chinese art?

Breckwoldt: I do not think so. The Chinese who worked with me were pleased because I used their ornaments and I created Chinese chairs more comfortable.

Watt: Are you sure you were not on a mission to develop a German development in furniture to be introduced into China?

Breckwoldt: No, I had to deal with German customers too. There was a big community and they were my customers.

Henchman: German customers got a reduced rate for the work you did?

Breckwoldt: No. I could not make it cheaper because the Chinese were starting to copy my models.

All in a time of war; all in a time of heightened tensions. But these lawyers, who had either avoided the war or were too old for it, were relishing their one-sided combat with a captive German. They asked whether Holm had designed any buildings with gymnasiums in them, to make sure he was not polluting the Australian physique with any notion of Aryan perfectionism. They were also certain he was surreptitiously trying to introduce German modernism into Australian architecture.

Holm's First World War experience was further evidence that he was now a spy planted in Australia. He had been a forward scout in the mounted cavalry on the Russian front. He crossed a frozen river at night on a railway bridge to report on the enemy's position and strength but was unable to return via that route because it had been blocked by Russian troops. He rode along the river in Russian-held territory until he came to this trestle bridge, which he rode his horse across. For that he was awarded Germany's Iron Cross and promoted to lieutenant.

He once told me, in the only war story he ever related, that if he had tried to lead the horse across the bridge on foot the animal would not have been as alert as it was when he rode it across, stepping from one sleeper to the next. And with no horse he might not have survived. Today, I fully appreciate his reasoning: a riderless horse will balk at a challenge it will accomplish with ease when directed to do so by a confident rider.

Then there was the matter of Angela's Heil Hitlers. Their former landlords at Darling Point, Mr and Mrs Skinner, were willing witnesses before the committee. They had seen young Angela perform a Heil Hitler in the back seat of their car when they took my parents and her on a picnic. The fact that the princesses Elizabeth and Margaret, who were much older than Angela, were doing their proficient Heil Hitlers at this very same time on the other side of the world was probably unknown to the advisory committee. No doubt the infant Angela had seen other Germans, perhaps her mother and father, mock Hitler—or indeed, as events will show, she may have witnessed more serious versions by Germans in Australia who hoped Germany would win the war. Whatever the case, clearly three-year-old Angela was a disciple of the devil Hitler.

The Skinners also reported that my parents had burned some paper in the backyard, which the committee concluded was a sign of them destroying incriminating evidence. Holm responded that they were simply getting rid of accumulated rubbish before moving to Bondi. The committee placed great weight on the testimony of the Skinners, one of whose allegations was reproduced in the committee's report as 'It was alleged that the objector's wife used the words "English swine" when referring to British colonial possessions'.

In their report the committee concluded that Holm was 'an intelligent type, with military experience and training, who still professes love for his country and still has relations living there'. Consequently, in view of all the material presented to them, they said he should remain interned.

That left Mum and Angela alone in the Bondi flat without any means of support. Blinds were drawn and only one light allowed. Outside the night sky was streaked with searchlights. Bondi Beach was a war zone, with rolls of barbed wire between sand and sea and its promenade fitted with tank traps. Locals nicknamed these obstacles The Maze and soon learned how to pick their way through it for a swim in the clear, uncluttered ocean.

Mum considered her options. Among them was the offer of food and lodgings in a convent for the entire duration of the war. This was not taken up, but it was the reason Angela eventually went to Our Lady of Mercy Convent in Parramatta, where Mum later taught the nuns German. But in Sydney on 30 March 1942 she went to police headquarters and demanded to be interned along with Holm.

Mum threatening a tantrum was intimidating enough; in full meltdown she was truly spectacular. She could prostrate herself on the floor in a flash, she could throw everything within reach and break it while banging her head up and down with uncontrollable wailing as if to end her life.

The police on this occasion would not have experienced her at full throttle, but they would no doubt have sensed trouble ahead from the way she said: 'I am a good German and I think it will be far better if you intern me now, before I do and say things which will cause you to rush and intern me. As a good German, my place is with my husband in an internment camp, which holds no terrors for me. Although I am a very sick woman, and my child is not very strong.'

There you go—that bloody 'good German' thing again, and that is not the last of it.

Mum was given the opportunity for an appeal but declined as she had volunteered. All official, of course, as the certificate stamped '30 September 1943, Reg. No. 11407' states that NF. 1681- BRECKWOLDT, Ilse (German) did not desire to do so.

I am memory free of internment. Angela, who was there from the ages of three to seven, remembers it clearly and it had a dreadful impact on her. Today we know about refugees held in detention and the traumatic results it had on them and their children. Some care about that, but not enough do. Far fewer cared about the internment of good citizens during the Second World War. Angela walked up to one of the guards at Moorebank and said she would promise not to run away if they took the barbed wire down. She was terrified by their bayonets, deciding at that tender young age that she would rather be shot than stabbed.

It was not long before Holm, Mum and Angela found they were about to be transferred by train from Moorebank to

Tatura in Victoria, where there was a complex of internment camps. Tatura was regarded as a perfect location for internment because it was in a rural area and a long way inland for any escapees to make it to a city or seaport.

To get from Moorebank to Sydney's Central Station, they sat on low seats in the back of a Land Rover troop carrier that travelled fast at night without headlights because of the blackout. It hit a bank and rolled. Angela emerged with a bleeding nose and a sore back, which she blames for problems that linger to this day. She fretted over the welfare of Pepiermarty, a canary they had managed to keep all that time. Holm assured her Pepiermarty would be fine but, without any birdseed and a diet of bread and water, it died on the train before reaching Tatura.

Their new domain, Camp 3 for German Families, was in the grip of a drought; dust storms ripped across a bleak, flat landscape. Angela was convinced they were in a desert. There were no animals, but once a guard brought his dog in. The crowd of internees around that dog was so deep that Angela could not get near it. Sometimes snakes breached the barbed wire, but they induced fear instead of interest.

2

THE BAR-BED-WIRE KID

When I did happen, it was without a sound. The walls of the one-room dormitories were composed of single sheets of Masonite. Except for a whisper, everything said could be heard and could provide all sorts of entertainment to those next door. There were no double beds, so Holm and Mum pulled their creaky iron beds next to each other. Angela slept beside them in her cot.

My birth was a precise military procedure. There was a fully functioning hospital in the internment camps, but the family myth goes that they wanted me born in the town of Tatura so I would become a British citizen, the status of all Australians at the time.

Regardless, my birth certificate, dated 8 February 1944, states that I was born at Waranga Military Hospital, Tatura. My parents' 'place of residence' is Number 3 Internment Camp, Tatura. My father's age is fifty-two, my mother thirty-three, and Angela seven. The 'informant' on my birth certificate is Lieutenant E.K. Horwood, Intelligence Officer, Number 1 Camp, Tatura. The mother is usually the informant, but Horwood was ascribed this position due to my mother being an internee and therefore incompetent of knowing she had given birth. The witnesses to my illustrious birth are Major Perrins, Australian Army Medical Corps and Sister Heaphy, Australian Army Nursing Service.

Later, Mum would excuse any of my frequent delinquencies with 'Poor boy, he can't help it, he was born behind bar-bed wire'. 'Barbed wire' in one flow was beyond Mum's German tongue. As was fish and chips, by the way, which she pronounced 'fish and ships', much to the consternation of the Greek proprietor in Parramatta, engaged in his own battle with the English language. But her bar-bed-wire excuse for my bad behaviour, now I come to think about it, was like a small anchor—one that could be easily dragged to conveniently excuse both her and me.

Mum, you will have gathered, belonged to the nurture school; for her, my environment explained everything. Handy that. My father conflated nurture and nature in tuning my good German blood to reach perfection. I would like to say he achieved his objective, but things got in the way. My name, for starters.

Can you imagine a freshly minted Australian-born baby called Roland Johannes Breckwoldt? Why not Darrell, Shane or Ray? Set me up for success. I am with Johnny Cash and his boy named Sue. Of course, exchanging Breckwoldt for Brown was out of the question, but there were plenty of heavy mid-European accents getting around after the war as Curtis or Powell. A Brakewell could have joined them, which is how most people pronounced and spelled Breckwoldt anyway.

I learned to live with Roland and its many convenient iterations. I still give my name slowly and clearly to operators at the NRMA or Telstra call centres, who then politely ask: 'May I call you by your first name, Ronald?' But I hated the Johannes part. Right from day one, I reckon.

I was about forty-five before I summoned the courage to murder him. The clerk in the sheriff's office at the Bega Courthouse, who I consulted about my intended deletion, said, 'Simplest thing, mate, just don't use it.' I applied his advice with a passion beyond your comprehension. But try out the modest removal of a middle name when you apply for a passport, a driver's licence or anything that relates to officialdom. 'Are you Roland Breckwoldt, or Roland Johannes Breckwoldt?' All too hard.

So Johannes survived, although absent or hidden under 'John' on the qualification certificates I managed to obtain later in life. They hang in my office to remind me of my insecurity as much as my achievement. Maybe the insecurity drove me to them. I often wonder about that, and what other destinations insecurity took me to.

Boredom was a big issue in the internment camps, and the men looked forward to being on a work roster that involved tasks such as collecting wood outside the camp or attending the big vegetable garden within it. One day Holm returned from work duty badly beaten up by a group of Nazi sympathisers. Mum told Angela he had fallen off a chair.

The result, but not the reason, is recorded in Casualty Form for N 1579 Breckwoldt stating that he was treated at Waranga Military Hospital, Tatura on 13 January 1943 and returned to the camp being, and I quote from the report, 'Marched in ex Hospital on 15 January 1943'.

Just as contemporary prisons are often controlled by gangs operating under the control system, there were Nazis in the internment camps that hoped for a German victory. There were 399 German sailors rescued from the sunken cruiser *Kormoran* after its historic battle off Western Australia with the HMAS *Sydney*, which also sank but with the loss of all lives. Their officers were held nearby in the rural mansion Dhurringile, and they were permitted to wear their uniforms and to exchange the Nazi salute among themselves. Knowing that these sailors and their officers were nearby was probably an inspiration to Nazi sympathisers in the other camps.

Holm and Mum were called '*schwein* Germans' and they frequently had rocks thrown at their door. Angela knew the culprits and returned fire with rocks, powered by a determination that compensated for her size. Mum scolded her, saying, 'We don't do things like that,' and made Angela go and apologise. Angela still feels and talks about the humiliation. Perhaps Mum's overreaction was a result of their insecurity.

Angela started school in the internment camp. Her class was taught by a German missionary nun who had been among the Germans in Papua New Guinea and interned lest they corroborate with the Japanese. What was once 'German New Guinea' had become an Australian protectorate after the First World War. The nun told the class how the missionaries had tried to reduce cannibalism by importing tinned protein such as corned beef as a substitute for human muscle and sinew. The cans were appropriately labelled with a cow. The sources of other tinned products were also clearly illustrated, such as beans with a bean label, but they had to stop importing the tinned baby food because it showed a baby on the tin.

Meanwhile, Holm turned the entrance to their one-room dormitory into a vine-covered trellis. Under it was an old tub he had scrounged and filled with some water plants with yabbies he had collected while out on work duty. The yabbies and their water had been carried in two buckets slung under a yoke fashioned with scrounged timber and rope. Holm had seen that form of carriage powered by peasant muscle and bone in China and Japan; now he was one of them. He also employed his artistic skills by drawing portraits of the guards, for which he received small favours or items such as an immersible water heater that provided warm water for washing or heating my milk.

Despite their differences, there was also some camaraderie among the internees. The men would save some of their ration of bread and dried fruit to feed a still that produced schnapps. The general diet consisted mainly of cabbage and meat, but the freshly cooked bread they received was excellent. That induced my father to create a piece of artwork that hung in the mess that contained exquisite hand-lettering proclaiming, with biblical fervour, 'Give Us Our Daily Bread'.

The tide of war began to turn against Germany not long after my birth. The daily roll call relaxed to a weekly event and the guards did less guarding. On one occasion they took male internees out on a hunting trip and provided each of them with a rifle and ammunition for the occasion. True. Holm was one of them, and they went outside the camp into the rural surrounds to shoot rabbits. He managed to shoot a hare and bragged to Mum that it was far superior to the rabbits shot by others.

Imagine the official camp logbook: 'To meet Camp Strategic Plan Goal 1, *Improving Staff-Inmate Relations*, a group of male internees were taken on a hunting trip outside the camp and issued with rifles and ammunition for that purpose.' Hardly likely. All unofficial, no doubt, but an example of how things were changing both inside the camp and in the world beyond it.

This encouraged my parents to apply for release in February 1945. It was refused by the Director General of Security in Canberra, who presented a comprehensive summary of the report made by the committee that had heard Holm's original appeal.

Then, just one month later, my parents were granted an interview with Flight Lieutenant Philcox, who must have been the first person with any empathy and understanding of their situation. Having listened to them, his conclusion was: 'These people will serve their own interests first. They realize that there is no hope for Germany and are anxious to stay in Australia and make the best of their prospects here.'

This was a major step for Philcox to take as the war had not yet ended (it would run for another five months). I have tried to track him down but I couldn't find an official record of his tenure and position. His report resulted in Holm being released on 14 May 1945 on the condition that he find work and accommodation for his family. It was a form of parole.

Holm contacted people he had worked for prior to internment. One referred him to Dr Wearne, a dentist who owned an extensive estate of over 350 acres at North Rocks on the north-western fringe of Sydney. Wearne had a small vacant cottage on a piggery on which it was agreed Holm would do repairs in exchange for rent.

Security agent H.H. Mortlock interviewed Holm at the cottage on 6 August 1945 and wrote a scathing report to the Deputy Director of Security for New South Wales, stating that Holm had made no progress in repairing the cottage and his release should be reviewed. The report concluded with: 'BRECKWOLDT asked that his wife be given at least a week's notice of intention to release her and the children to give her time to pack. BRECKWOLDT did not impress me as being sincere, either in regard to obtaining suitable accommodation for his family or for their early release.'

Despite that report, Mum, Angela and I were released five months later, allowing us to proceed to North Rocks and take up life on the piggery. We each had official revoking orders. At one year of age my status remained uncertain. The National Security (General) Regulation Revoking Detention Order described me as 'NM.1681(a) Roland Breckwoldt who was detained at an unspecified date'.

The 'unspecified date' is curious, given they knew the exact date of my birth. Maybe I had become a danger when I was returned to the camp a few days after I was born. More likely, there was so much documentation on us that no one bothered to check my birth date.

'I like this bloody place,' exclaimed Mum when she arrived at the piggery. Her vernacular was an early indication of how well she would adapt to Australia and it allayed Holm's fears that she would refuse to live in the piggery. That is the reason he had been so reluctant to do much work on it, which had resulted in the unfavourable security report.

Angela thought it was heaven, with plum trees and baby pigs to look at. Holm quickly had the little fibro shack covered in flowering vines and it soon looked like a home.

~

The piggery houses my first memory. There is a lizard in a jar on the windowsill next to my cot in that tiny fibro cottage that had been caught and jarred by Holm when I was about two. Through the mist of what I want to see I make it a jacky lizard with twin stripes down its back. An *Amphibolurus muricatus,* also known as a twin-striped lizard, in case you want to know, and resembling a small and nimble version of a bearded dragon. I apply that taxonomy because my captive lizard was different to the abundant small skinks that crawled around outside. Chances are that my jacky lizard was ultimately released from its jar. If it wasn't, I rationalise its unfortunate demise as a sacrifice to my lifelong interest in reptiles.

Family photos were rare then. Too much trouble having to buy film at the chemist's, then carrying around a cumbersome Box Brownie camera before having to take the film back to Parramatta to get developed and back again to pick up the photos. But in one shoebox survivor, I am about four and standing at the edge of a rock above Lake Parramatta in the background, my legs apart in that stance of the young and confident. I am wearing a straw cowboy hat and have a long rope looped in my left hand and a lasso noose in my right hand. I could have lassoed the world ahead of me, and perhaps I did. Later, I told anyone asking about my life choices that 'I was always that way.' It was straightforward, plausible enough and said without awareness that I was claiming a big slice of life for myself.

Having renounced German nationality and attained five years of residency during the four years in the internment camp, my parents and Angela were granted British citizenship on 29 August 1946. My status was finally resolved and showed that I am true blue, but with an English bent. No 'good German' was apparent in me; I was on the other team now. The certification informed my parents: 'It will be observed that the name of your Australian born child is not included in the Certificate. The reason for the omission is that as the child was born in Australia he is a British subject by birth.'

British citizens we were, but some kids at North Rocks threw stones at us when we walked from the piggery, providing a visible demonstration of what their parents were saying behind closed doors. I was stroller-bound and oblivious. Angela told me that Holm would walk directly ahead, instructing her and Mum to do likewise without concern or retaliation. Sometimes they would be awakened at night by the sound of rocks landing on the corrugated-iron roof. Rock throwing had been directed at them in the internment camp by Nazi sympathisers, and now it was coming from Australians. Holm and Mum were outsiders again, part of the big displacement.

As newly minted British citizens, Holm and Mum were permitted to purchase a half-acre section of a cleared paddock on a short dirt road that contained a few houses and couple of orchards before petering into the bush. Holm began to conceive the house he wanted to build there. Nothing would be allowed to stand in the way of his concept of what Chinese gardens crossed with art nouveau and German ingenuity could bring to life on that little cow paddock.

It all started well. While we still lived at the piggery, he would put me in a little billycart and tow it behind him as he went off to work on the house about one kilometre away. I was then just over two years of age and he would encourage me by saying we were sure to uncover an *eidechse*, German for 'small lizard', under the sheets of fibro stacked ready for the house.

Holm built the house on his own, with a minor contribution by me. Fibro and corrugated iron were the building materials of the time, but even they were in scarce supply during the long, cold austerity after the war. Holm had fibro cutters with a cutting jaw in a big square head on the end of long handles. The timber window frames were painted with a red lead paint primer, then a pink undercoat and another two coats of exterior blue. No mask to protect against the fibro and no gloves against the red lead. I was soon handling both materials and was much too good at my work, which meant Holm was hatching bigger plans.

Some people have described me as mad. Mum blamed the bar-bed wire. I blame the countless hours I spent painting two coats of red lead, one coat of pink primer and two coats of blue paint on every window frame and sill on that fibro house.

Holm fashioned a rope harness for me to pull a wheelbarrow with him pushing at the handles. Together, we moved soil up from the backyard along a narrow alley between the house and boundary to convert the front yard into terraced gardens. My job included sifting each shovel-load of soil to remove the weeds. I would take out a corm of onion grass, which we knew as 'plum pudding', and with great deliberation would throw it as far as I could. Holm soon put a stop to that by getting me to fill an empty jam tin, before he would carefully discard the contents, saying, 'Always be practical, son.'

The house ended up a friendly little place sitting on brick piers. Miraculously, it was soon decorated with Chinese antiques that had been stored all those years by a Good Samaritan who remains unknown to me. There were two bedrooms: one for our parents, the other for the children. A microscopic kitchen, because it was for women only. All connected to a small lounge area that contained a formal dining table by a long and wide room with big sliding windows, through which I could watch the world. This room held a small marble table at which we ate most meals. The big disadvantage was that all the rooms were connected by a wooden floor that required someone getting on their hands and knees and applying Wundawax in voluminous quantities before applying equal amounts of physical energy to transform it into a polished floor. No need to tell you whose job that was.

~

North Rocks was more of a connection than a place at that time. North Rocks Road took the easy route along a low ridge that fell gently away to creeks on either side. Every wet gully fed creeks that were caught by Darling Mills Creek, which formed part of the border with Baulkham Hills and emptied its dose of dye and waste from the Sydney Woollen Mills into the Parramatta River, the great collector that connected us to the sea.

The bus route to Parramatta railway station passed the high sandstone walls of Parramatta Gaol. Passengers on the red and yellow Watson and Hume bus, cocooned on brown leather seats imprinted with circles made by thick metal spring coils, were unaware that those sandstone blocks had been originally quarried by levelling a spectacularly tall sandstone tower-like cliff, from which North Rocks had derived its name. Here was beauty transferred to a prison. We Breckwoldts were heading in the opposite direction.

Holm started his privacy campaign by planting deodar trees close together just inside the boundary around the front garden. He was always an outsider and could never become anyone else. The barriers he erected were an extension of himself, and he put us all inside there with him. He built a big wooden gate that contained a small opening for daily use; the big gate never swung properly and was just in case larger landscaping or building materials needed to enter. He planted mulberry trees all around our backyard boundary. The Breckwoldt inner sanctum was underway, and the deodar and mulberry trees never looked back, a dense barrier to the outside world.

German was my first language. Holm and Mum had become very competent in English, but we had to speak German at home. Mum was more flexible and did not mind if some English got mixed with the German. Holm was adamant that all communication be in German. Any English would result in another ear-grabbing with a stern: '*Vas ist das, Rrr-rorlant? Ich kann nicht verstehen.*' (What's that, Roland? I cannot understand.)

German spoken quietly at home was bearable, but there was no escape from Holm's German on the bus or anywhere in public. He set the decibels high enough to let everyone know he remained proud and uncrushed. He could, however, whenever convenient switch between being a German and an Austrian. I avoided going with him on that bus and it lasted well into my high school years. If he got off work early and I spotted him at the bus station, I would disappear before he saw me and wait an hour for the next bus.

We were living a German life in Australia in the shadow of a concluded war. Attention was unavoidable, but nothing was done to ameliorate it. Holm loved the beach, partly for swimming and partly for observing young women brave enough to start wearing two-piece swimsuits. He never missed the chance to go on Watson and Hume bus specials for the carless people of North Rocks to go to the beach. Passengers sang along to 'Daisy, Daisy (give me an answer do)' and 'Goodnight Irene' to fill the journey across Frenchs Forest to Mona Vale, but Holm never joined in, sitting silently looking out the window, unable to disguise his wilful disengagement from such commonness. I wanted to join in, but I was afraid to sing lest I offend him and he rebuked me in public, probably in German loud enough to be heard by everyone from the driver to the back row.

Holm was swimming against the tide long before we got to the beach; that was his default position. Being and staying different meant so much to him, but it left me squirming between two worlds. The only benefit might have been that I was learning, without appreciating the lesson, that it is possible to march to a different drummer and survive. I knew none of that then. I did not know what resilience was. I did not even know what question was being asked of Daisy or why saying goodnight to Irene was such a big deal.

The hardening of young Roland began early. When I try to trace my hardening, I put the 'nigger boy' event as the earliest I can remember. He was my dearly beloved little black boy childhood comfort doll. Blissfully ignorant that his name would become marred by its racist origins, we were inseparable until I forgot him on a sandstone platform beside a creek winding between moss and maidenhair fern. The hairy goblin seed pods on an old *Banksia serrata* saw it all; I wish they had spoken up. Distracted, playing in the creek, catching tadpoles and looking for yabbies, I left without my comfort doll.

Almost home, I begged and pleaded with Holm for us to go back and get him. He steadfastly refused. I asked Mum to come back with me next morning to retrieve him, but no luck there; she had other things to do. I suspect the disappearance of my comfort doll was manufactured by one or both my parents because they had decided I was too old for such a need.

A bearded dragon became my instant new friend. I caught it in our backyard and took it to my cot in the room I shared with Angela and spent day and night playing with it. I am not sure what pleasure the bearded dragon derived from my play, but it was not averse to the attention and ate freely from scraps of mincemeat. Angela recalls that I took my bearded dragon to bed with me every night and carried it either on my shoulder or under my jumper all day long. She told me that me and my dragon were inseparable. I have no memory at all of this, but apparently Mum refused to let me take it on the bus for shopping in Parramatta and I secreted it under my jumper. It emerged at the Commonwealth Bank, where it created wonderment among staff and customers. Doubtless I enjoyed the attention and it fed my infatuation with reptiles. I learned how to get jobs done quickly and lived for playing in the surrounding quilt of bush and farmland. I looked for lizards at first and snakes later.

'German sausage' and 'hamburger' regularly emerged from the mouths of kids, who could only have learned it from their parents as they discussed the Breckwoldts behind closed doors. I was only about four when Bruce Hudson kicked me hard in the backside. His daughter, Barbara, and I had had an entirely accidental collision on a rough swing that hung from a branch and had the lid of a fruit box as its seat. She ran home crying and he came back with her to really hurt me with a full adult-sized kick. He was a returned soldier and might have enjoyed kicking a German.

A serious charge of assault today, but I did not even tell my parents in case they were angry with me too. That was the start of me keeping things to myself. Being kicked up the arse by a big bullying man was really upsetting.

A good rock fight with Barbara's cousins, twins John and Barry Hudson, always helped me deal with resentment. I had learned how to throw rocks in the womb, and with Holm's strength training I was a talented rapid-fire and deadly accurate rock thrower. My experience in the bush meant I could quickly assess the best-sized rock out of the extensive ammunition available along the dirt road. Once I hit Barry so hard in the chest with a decent-sized rock he fell to the ground. How we did not take out each other's eyes or teeth in our many rock fights is merely good fortune; imagine the kick the German brat would have got for a sunken eye!

I was constantly reminded of another Australia by the Webbs next door. The Saturday night quiet would be broken every now and then when the Webbs gathered around their pianola with friends and relatives to sing late into the night. I could hear it all and I really liked it, and I wanted to be around that pianola with the aunts, uncles and cousins. Any relatives I had were on the other side of the world and were very rarely mentioned, let alone talked about. Mum liked to say her father was a doctor and to make an occasional mention of the family farm in Schleswig-Holstein.

Mum was also capable of delivering extreme embarrassment. She took 'bar-bed-wire' and 'fish and ships' to an entirely new level during a visit to Taronga Zoo. We came to the koala enclosure, where four or five of them dozed in the midday sun, drugged dead to the world on their morning feast of eucalypt leaves. To Mum they looked sullen and uncooperative. No way had she come all the way on bus, train and ferry to see sleeping koalas.

She noticed half a house brick lying nearby and picked it up in one hand and hurled it at the nearest koala, to shock it from doze to mobility. There were loud gasps of horror from the many assembled viewers. Her missile, too heavy to reach any koala, hit the concrete floor with a mighty thud, spraying broken fragments before rattling across the floor with what sounded to me like the sound of rolling thunder. I instantly melted into the crowd and pretended I did not know this wild woman.

Two other events I can still clearly recall. I was playing in a puddle in the middle of the road when Mr Schultz came around the corner and ran over me in his new Plymouth. I was knocked over, and I remember looking up and seeing the underneath of his car going over me. Had I been under one of his tyres this book would not have been written. Then, at about the age of four, I was busily using an old cricket stump to open out a neat little hole in the bracken on the nature strip outside our front gate when a big black snake, which had been residing in it, decided to evacuate by slithering across my hand.

Clearly, I survived it all: the growing up and the growing down without knowing it. In the end it was the outside world that captured me, leaving the rest of me untuned.

3

THE BEAUTIFUL QUILT

The orchards and dairies along North Rocks Road were perched on the very edge of the fertile Cumberland Plain before it fell into the craggy Hawkesbury sandstone. Gullies of bush crept up and grasped at the farms. Those gullies fed creeks that filled Lake Parramatta, my teenage retreat. Its cold, deep water was held inside a high curved wall made of huge sandstone blocks convicts had carved and cemented to lean into it. Parramatta's water supply when it was the cradle of Australian agriculture. To me as a child it marked the south-western end of my mental map. To the north was Carlingford and between them lay what seemed to be an endless stretch of bush that was unmeasurable to us.

The farmers at North Rocks never ventured into the bush; I suppose they got their fix of outdoors on their farms. They were small producers in a shaky symbiosis with the city they fed, which grew so fast it would soon eat their farms. The older farms had weatherboard houses sitting squarely where they were meant to be. No big homesteads, nothing grand. Some of the builders, mechanics, plumbers and truck drivers had a paddock or a bush block they did not do much with. Unused paddocks soon sprouted bracken, melaleuca, acacia and blackthorn in anticipation of a more concerted invasion by eucalypts, producing a rich quilt of battle between bush and farm.

Scattered among them were the Italian vegetable growers, who leased small sections of the unused paddocks then converted tin sheds into homes. The older generation among them had been captured in North Africa and sent to Tatura, in a camp right next to ours. Mussolini's and Hitler's collateral damage were now side by side at North Rocks, putting their lives back together. The Italians worked hard on those market gardens, and beginning from 1953, just eight years after the war ended, they could sponsor relatives from Italy to create extended families and increase their workforce. Suddenly our primary school classes marked the change, with much older Italian children in attendance because they could not speak English.

The Italians never went into the bush. Any bird bigger than a blue wren was for eating. Fortunately, the favourite avian addition to their diet was the feral Indian turtle dove, which they dispatched with their .410 shotguns. Mum would send me off to them with one of her shoulder baskets and two shillings to buy vegetables plucked straight from their market gardens. They, like us, held on to their language and I always thought they were having heated domestics when I heard their voices raised in animated gesticulation.

The bush took our family into its warm, welcoming envelope. The further into the bush I ventured the safer I became. Holm was the leader here and I thank him for it. He had that schizophrenic German relationship that balanced order and wilderness, which would show up as he walked along faint tracks and broke off protruding branches as he went without even a pause in his pace. Sometimes Mum came along, and they would admire the lemon-scented boronia in patches of delicate pink under eucalypts that blended into turpentine, shading a creek winding under honeycombed sandstone.

A state government–imposed green belt, modelled on illusory visions of green cities somewhere in England, prevented too much subdivision. We were part of those who slipped through the net as some farms were permitted to cut off a block here and there. Those of us who got to love the bush thought it had resilience in its vastness, but that left it without advocates. There would be no sleep under the patchwork quilt that so enriched my childhood.

That became my territory, and by age six I was exploring the sandstone overhangs that housed clusters of finely daubed mud swallow nests with narrow entry tunnels. We called them 'bottle-neck swallows' because 'fairy martin' lay outside our vocabulary. Ring-tailed possums stripped bark for their nests from turpentine trees in the gullies that fed a big creek. That creek pooled deeply in front of wide, flat sandstone reefs pitted with perfectly rounded, deep, pebble-eroded holes before tumbling over waterfalls. Flat Rock became my second home . . . on reflection, maybe my first home.

My friend Robbie and I dog-paddled in a deep, dark, tannin-stained section banked up in front of the rock face that had blocked it up for a while. Not far from it, and almost leaning over the creek, was our double-decker cave, which had been formed from a rock face that fell and left a passage behind and above it. Robbie and I made fires in that passage; we toasted white bread and coughed on 'cigarettes' of rolled newspaper.

The McCanns were the first Australians to make us welcome, and while I was in their home and backyard I was safe from any derogatory remarks about Germans. Mrs McCann's sister had married an Italian wool buyer based in Sydney, which may have made them more open to take people at face value even if their country of origin had been the enemy. I was taken into the McCann home and Robbie's room was as if my own. His parents bought him Phantom and Donald Duck comics, which we read before we began building cranes and spinning wheels out of his Meccano set so as to wind up the silk thread from our silkworm cocoons. Mrs McCann made us lunch and occasionally invited me to their Sunday roast.

The McCanns took me with them on a wonderful holiday to Patonga, where I fished off the jetty with Robbie from daylight to dark. It was one of the very few holidays I ever went on, as Mum and Holm never went on a holiday together during their entire lives. Later, Holm's clients Elaine and Larry Adler had me for holidays in the house he designed for them at Blakehurst. Kind, indeed, were those people.

Robbie and I roamed freely, while other parents protected their children from the dangerous bush and me. Robbie was a year younger than me but that made no difference in our predilections for adventure. He also had a father who made things. Mr McCann spent his working week commuting in army uniform to his position as a clerk at Victoria Barracks. He played Gilbert and Sullivan on his piano and it calmed their house. Like Holm, he lived for his weekends, but rather than gardening he made furniture and household fittings in his neat workshop with electrical saws, lathes and drills. This attracted Holm's attention without any friendship developing between them, but Mum and Mrs McCann became good friends.

Robbie and I crafted catapults, carefully selecting just the right-sized fork from a patch of young melaleuca regrowth in a thicket behind Bill McGuinness's orchard, from where we ogled his ripening nectarines and peaches. We had a particular penchant for a lone apple tree just across his fence.

Those catapults were little works of art. We constructed them in many variations, based on the size of the fork and the width of the rubber we cut from discarded car tubes. A tiny fork and thin rubber would be for carrying concealed in a pocket, to be used surreptitiously in the school playground and for impressing your friends. Then there were the big ones, which we hung around our necks. We were deadly shots at fixed targets, but sparrows and starlings evaded our attempts to dislodge them from gutters and roofs. For them, we eyed off the air rifles owned by kids older than us until such time as we could save enough money to buy our own.

I started getting attracted to keeping animals. It probably began with that lizard I kept in the jar and then grew further from our walks in the bush. Holm and Mum rarely got in the way of anything I turned up with. Holm never actively encouraged me to keep an extensive menagerie of pets but neither did he discourage me, apart from dogs and cats on which he put a limit of one at a time. I knew he had wealthy industrialist parents who were so remote during his childhood that he was without any memory of sitting on his father's knee.

Angela told me long after Holm died that a schoolfriend had given him a pair of white mice, but when he arrived home with them his father made him drown them in a jar of water. I had no soft feelings for Holm, but on hearing that and reflecting on it, I believe he wanted to act differently with me so he indulged my interest in animals. The twist is that I was turning to animals because they were much safer than people.

Reptiles were my favourites and to these were added ring-tailed possums, until a whole menagerie of domestic animals eventually occupied our backyard. White rabbits, guinea pigs, pigeons, white mice and budgerigars were added to the ring-tailed possums and many lizards.

Some of the cages I manufactured myself out of discarded fruit boxes, which in those days were made of wood. Other animals spent time in a low chook shed Holm built next to the outside toilet, which had an oval window that was high enough for me to be able to see over the chooks and view the world outside while sitting on that smelly toilet. I had chooks and ducks and, in a roundabout way, I created my own little farm.

I drooled over a young Australian falcon that Russell Meehan's father brought home from his army job at the

Holsworthy Barracks. Russell was regarded by everyone as backward and remained at the very edge of our lives because of his disability, but he was deeply adored by his father, who wrapped his life around him. One day Russell grabbed my bike and rode off on it. Mr Meehan was about to give chase to rescue it when I said, 'Don't worry about it, he can ride it as long as he likes.'

The next day Mr Meehan arrived at our house with the falcon in its cage and said to Mum, 'This is for Roland for his kindness to Russell.' I kept the falcon for a couple of months then set it free, which I did with all the native animals I kept throughout my childhood. I think about that now and remind myself that, among the bad, I did some good. As you'll find out, I am a sucker for the guilts.

Robbie and I always walked past the Driscoll house to get to the bush. We rarely saw Mrs Driscoll, and her sons Terry and Ian were much older and unknown to us. Mr Driscoll often got off the bus very drunk and staggered down the street in full song. Holm, who only drank the occasional small glass of sherry, held Mr Driscoll in contempt, but I secretly admired him because he went spearfishing and had another life. This was expressed in the frame he had constructed of a half-finished canoe: every rib had been painstakingly steam curved and fixed along the side frame, meticulously held together by tiny brass nails as it hung there from the verandah rafters waiting for some sort of skin.

Mr Driscoll said it was going to get an aluminium cover. I was thinking something more romantic, like a cow hide. He eventually gave me that half-finished canoe and I was overjoyed to take it home and sling it between the bearers under our house. But nothing ever came of it because I didn't know what to do next, and it disappeared along with my childhood.

Ashley Bowerman was about two years younger than Robbie and me and was never allowed to accompany us on even the mildest venture. There is something of a gloss that the 1950s was a time of wide-ranging freedoms when parents worried less about stranger danger and fast traffic, but there were many parents who did not allow their children to go into the bush, and particularly not with me.

Claude Bowerman grew roses and vegetables just down the road, but he kept Ashley strictly apart from us. Ashley and his younger brother Barry often walked hand in hand down the road; they had to be each other's best friend. Ashley had heard about our double-decker cave, and Mr Law, their neighbour who lived in a big weatherboard house in an orchard, offered to take him down to Flat Rock and show him the cave. Unlike us, Mr Law, as the name might imply, was indeed a respectable orchardist.

Ashley tried to reach the cave via the steeply sloping rock face abutting a deep part of the creek. It was part of the tumble-down that had created the cave, and Robbie and I avoided it by coming around behind the cave on a faint track we had created. Ashley lost his footing and fell into the creek. Mr Law could not swim and ran the half kilometre to find Mr Driscoll at home. They both rushed back but it was all too late; Mr Driscoll dived to retrieve Ashley's body.

The death of Ashley Bowerman sent a deep sense of shock through our little neighbourhood. At least I think it did, because I can't recall any talk. Whatever the case, it hung with me.

Many decades later, when I was in my sixties, I was a father myself and a farmer on the far South Coast. I visited North Rocks Cemetery and found Ashley's lonely and unattended grave. Among unkempt long grass, its tilting headstone and engraved epitaph, now fading with age, failed to erase that terrible event from my memory. I looked up the white pages and rang every Bowerman in the Sydney region until I found Barry and learned he had acquired a new baby brother not long after Ashley's death.

The death of Ashley, due to his protective parenting, would shape me as a father. I let my son Dan do stuff, use knives, climb trees, use an axe. Always a word of caution and some instruction, if appropriate, but rarely a no.

Angela told me that after Mr Sim tried to kill a brown snake, I crawled under the Sims' house to determine whether the snake had been duly dispatched. I was ten at the time. I found the snake very much alive and took it home to keep in a box in our bedroom. We all shared that tiny bedroom and Chris, who was about three, still recalls his fear of the snake.

Angela, who was then seventeen, is convinced it was a brown snake. Somewhere in my memory it was a yellow-faced whip snake, which is only partly venomous and has small fangs placed well to the rear of its mouth. It strikes me as strange that my strict and stern father neither encouraged nor discouraged my reptile keeping. It had to be the white mice event.

Whether brown snake or whip snake, the fact that I was not bitten does not surprise me. There are many cases of young kids picking up highly venomous snakes and not getting bitten because of the gentle way they handled them. Many years later I caught a white-lipped snake for my five- and eight-year-old nephews. We passed around this small, only slightly venomous snake for quite a while, letting it slide gently through our hands. We then placed it in a large jar to show their father and my brother-in-law Louis.

Louis was handed the same snake, and it bit him twice on the hand so fast you could hardly discern its movement. There was panic abroad, but my assessment was that Louis was a big, strong fellow who would hardly be affected and that a trip to the hospital in Bega would be a total waste of time. I was regarded by our respective wives as uncaring and lacking empathy. Notwithstanding my shortcomings, Louis survived the event with only minor swelling around the bites.

No house was complete unless it had a lawn front and back. The fact that we never owned a lawnmower was no impediment to that firm conviction, but Holm was not a push-mower type; he never purchased or obtained through other means any tool or motor with moving parts. The first petrol Victa mowers were becoming available but their cost was not in the plan, and the noise and maintenance would have irritated him. There was no need anyway because I was his perfect moving part. He reckoned I could achieve anything with a small sickle, provided he was the project director. The front lawn, after it was cut with my sickle, was not pretty, but that did not seem to interfere with his views over it to the garden beyond.

The back lawn, which was larger, was more of a challenge. Ray Spence always had a young lamb he was rearing for sale; it would mysteriously disappear when it got older and be replaced by another juvenile. Ray told me he had an uncle who took him to the Flemington saleyards, where he would be given a lamb born overnight from a ewe destined for the nearby Homebush abattoir. I longed for an uncle who would take me to the Flemington saleyards. Angela took me there, but I was too terrified to climb up above the crowded pens and walk along the high, narrow raised walkway between them. We returned lambless.

A sheep of some kind seemed a good alternative mower for our backyard lawn, which was running rampantly to seed with paspalum, cobbler's pegs and the aptly named weed, lamb's tongue. Mum obtained a large merino ram from one of her friends; he was no gentle, half-grown, rubber-teat-and-bottle-reared poddy but a fully mature ram, with his equipment dangling low among the grass. He had large curled horns separated by a bony forehead as hard as plate steel and an undercarriage of balls the size and shape of large mangoes, each with a little bare patch where it hit the ground after swinging wide as he walked.

The complete package needed an equally grand name and he became Horatio. I have no idea where that name came from; probably from Lord Horatio Nelson of the Battle of Trafalgar. We did have our battle with Horatio.

Horatio was kept on a tether long enough to cover a lot of the lawn, which meant he could also gather pace when his frustrations got the better of him. He would lower his horns and charge the nearest person, hitting them with his bony forehead so as to get his anger out of his system. Such was the case when he knocked the unsuspecting Chris halfway across the lawn, but most of the time Horatio was easy to manage. There was enough moisture in the grass to not have to water him regularly, and the long tether meant he could cover a lot of the lawn without needing to be moved very often.

Horatio seemed content doing what merinos do—eat grass and grow wool. The grass-devouring bit went well, but it sped his wool-growing component. His fleece grew so long and luxuriant that even us novices knew he required shearing. North Rocks, being a long way from the wheat-sheep belt, was devoid of shearers and Mum came up with the novel idea that the big kitchen scissors would do the trick.

Mum went up to Horatio and waved the scissors at him, either to frighten or hypnotise him, but he did not comprehend the program so I steadied him by the horns while Mum went to work. The scissors worked well on his fine white merino wool hidden under its grey-matted exterior, but Mum's fingers couldn't keep going. She had blisters within minutes, with only a small bare patch on Horatio's back to show for it.

Holm was nowhere to be seen. He had too much faith in me and my sickle to take any interest in Horatio—it was only the back lawn anyway—so it was my turn with the scissors, but I got blisters and they burst. The scissors worked; we didn't.

After that initial foray into shearing my fingers required a school week to heal, so the shearing of Horatio became a weekend activity. It took about six weeks to shear him in two-hour sessions with our gradually hardening fingers. Although Horatio looked a fright, he tolerated it easily, as if enjoying the attention. Word got out and my friends came to watch in amusement.

~

Jeff Clark also occupies space in the backpack of my life. Clark, who lived with his wife and three daughters in a neat fibro house, was regarded as a good family and community man. He had some status through owning a combined florist and dry-cleaning business in Parramatta. On Sundays he gave his time and car to transport children to the Methodist Church Sunday school further down North Rocks Road. He was medium height, skinny and nondescript, but I saw him ride a horse once and I thought he looked good on it—but then, anyone on a horse looked good to me.

One early evening just on dusk when I was about nine, Mum asked me to deliver her coat to Clark for dry-cleaning. He was home alone and asked if I wanted to come in to watch television. To be invited inside to watch this invention that had come into special homes like this was beyond my expectations and I eagerly accepted, but after getting absorbed in watching Bob Dyer's *Pick a Box* quiz show for a few minutes, Clark suggested we go outside to view his budgerigar aviary. There did not seem much choice in the matter and I wanted to please him, so I followed him into the gathering dark and stood alongside him at the aviary.

Clark got very excited and explained how male and female budgerigars went about their mating ritual. His voice reached a higher pitch and his words sped while he began mimicking their behaviour with me as his model. He slipped around behind me to give me a practical demonstration of budgerigar mating behaviour. With both hands on my shoulders, he began pressing something hard into my shorts. I sensed this was only remotely associated with budgerigars, broke free and ran all the way home.

As with everything else, I kept it entirely to myself. Maybe I was anticipating disappointment, thinking that Holm or Mum would fail to confront Clark. I could also have done them a huge favour, as it would have been Clark's word against mine. Imagine the word of a good Australian family man and Christian Sunday school transporter against that of a nine-year-old German kid, already known for being a bit on the wild side.

Clark probably knew exactly what he was doing by picking on someone who was vulnerable and who would not be believed, and if Holm and Mum had taken the matter further they would have been ostracised and pushed further back into their German isolation, from which Mum at least was trying so hard to emerge. I can't calculate how Holm would have reacted, which was my problem. Clark may have expected an enraged visit by Holm and gone to bed with the returned wife and children, ready to deny it all.

My reaction to the encounter was one of total surprise. No shock, abhorrence, guilt or remorse, just surprise about what was hidden in that house. I had always thought our family had sole ownership of eccentricity. Perhaps Mrs Clark's doses of Bex, which she purchased daily at the local corner shop followed by long hours of gossip, told the fuller story. So naïve was I that I did not even wonder whether I was the only child who had been given the budgerigar treatment after the same or different introduction.

Years later, having made new friends at high school who lived near the Sunday school to which Clark ferried participants, I found the courage to tell them what he had tried to do to me. They laughed with, 'Didn't you know that? Everyone knows that.' That was the end of it. I should have asked how they knew that and how many others he may have molested.

Just to get things in perspective, I was not totally wild in my primary school days. The Karls were Dutch and lived two doors down from the Clarks. I babysat their two young daughters; they did not like to be constrained by time when they went out to party, so they would set me up with supper and a nice clean bed to sleep in. They always gave me ten shillings, a sizeable fortune, but the generous supper and a room of my own was the highlight. That was the other face of my wild side: the Karls knew I was competent and could be trusted to look after their children overnight, even though I was only eleven years old.

The nature strip on the corner of our street and North Rocks Road was the favoured location for an itinerant who visited each year for several years in a small truck with a canvas-enclosed tray, and then disappeared from our lives. The shoe repair man slept on a bunk among his tools and repaired shoes during the day. I sat around his kerosene lamp and listened to his stories of the road and would stay with him until he sent me home so he could get some sleep.

I nagged him for his name, but his reply would be the same every time: 'I am Uncle Tom and this is Uncle Tom's cabin.' Then he never came again.

4

HORSE DREAMING

Bonnie the draught horse stood high among Pop Maher's menagerie of chooks, ducks, geese and pigs, all of which lived in slab sheds among an orchard of plums, apricots and peaches. A dainty fawn Jersey milking cow ran with her calf in a little bush paddock with a creek by day and was brought in at night and separated from her calf so there was milk to be pulled in the morning.

Bonnie, a rich bay–coloured mare with a big white blaze, pulled a single-furrow plough between the rows of Pop's orchard so he could grow oats and corn for all those animal mouths. Pop's hands were totally occupied wrestling the ungainly plough, so the long rein in each hand was more for connection than control. Sometimes Bonnie pulled a dray, which was just a large, heavy-timbered box on skids. Depending on the state of my friendship with Pop's grandson Ray Spence, I got to sit in it for short rides. Bliss, intensified by rarity. It was a rural paradise ruled by a cranky old king.

Then there was Pop's wife, Nan. I am dead certain she did nothing else all year except make plum puddings, containing silver coins, that ripened while hanging from the rafters of the laundry, each in a meal-sized linen bag tied with string. They made such an impression on me because of my unrequited urge to taste one.

I never got to sample any of those puddings. Thrift was the key to survival on Pop's small farm, and that excluded an outsider like me from even a peach or apricot from the many, even if they had fallen to the ground. I might slip past the kitchen into Ray's bedroom on rare occasions but never sampled any of the bottles of dry ginger ale and lemonade stacked in crates under their house.

We kids picked freesia flowers growing wild along the roadside and gave them to our mothers' vases, but Ray picked them for Pop to sell at the markets. Everything had a value, and everything was for sale. The two native Christmas bushes jammed tight between the front of Pop's house and North Rocks Road were cropped within centimetres of their life each year when they flowered red in their short-lived glory. The family was frugal and must have talked about money, must have learned about managing it. Money was hush-hush in the fibro homes of the invaders such as us. Rude to ask, and spent secretly. Pop totally ignored me. He never said a word to me, let alone a friendly one.

The Maher mob consisted of three different families, and they huddled close together on land Pop had given them when they married. A remnant rural extended family surrounded by nuclear intruders, glued by family and the opportunity to occupy land in a little kingdom in which Pop was king.

Pop may have been a First World War veteran and there were probably sons-in-law just back from the Second World War. As the 'German kid', I was probably only tolerated because of my tenuous friendship with Ray, but there was always some tension about what you could do and where you could go to avoid Pop's ire. Ray liked to exert a bit of authority over me, but then he was probably almost as frightened of old Pop as I was.

One of Ray's cousins—she was eleven or twelve and seemed so old to me at eight—sternly advised me, 'Roland, you want to be the in-law and outlaw of everybody.' Deadly accurate, even if she did get it from Pop or Nan or others in that impenetrable family. I ached to belong and, without that, found my identity in what they knew as my wild side.

There was one member of that family who didn't ignore me: Billy Ryan, a nuggety wharfie who was married to one of Pop's daughters and loved playing dominoes with Ray and me. Billy was the benefactor of a house for the extended family. Billy's wife does not reside in my memory as she always faded away into the dark house, but the laughing and friendly Billy Ryan remains.

Our milk was delivered by Buddy and Russell Crosby in their shiny new dark green milk cart, pulled by a horse decked out in leather livery with brass buckles. The cart was decorated with scrolled stencilling and carried two milk vats, each with polished brass taps, enabling them to work both sides of the road in one pass. They filled the billycans that were left out with two shillings in them.

I would never go near their horse because Buddy and Russell called me a snicklegrub on sight. I did not have to know what 'snicklegrub' meant for it to put a gaping pit of hurt and pain in my stomach. I can laugh about that now, but it has been a long time coming. At the time it put me on the outside, even well beyond reach of myself. The chances are that my snicklegrub was a handy corruption of the name Schiklgruber that appears in Hitler's ancestry. If that is the case then the Crosbys were unlikely to be the originators, but I am the only known recipient.

Years later I got much closer to a gorgeous big thoroughbred stallion. Robbie and I had our favourite dams for catching carp with a worm threaded on a bent pin attached to cotton at the end of a bamboo rod. A slice of cork with a hole punched through it with a match allowed us to adjust the length of the line between float and hook. The dam that offered us the minimum waiting time for the cork to start bobbing and highest yield was just past one of Dr Wearne's rural cottages, which was vacant most of the year then quite suddenly occupied by a dapper-looking man and his stallion.

We were wary at first of this man who wore clothes so different to our parents. His checked cap over a clipped moustache and neatly pressed checked shirt and fawn jodhpurs made him more military than familiar. There was a big stallion hanging about too, and we kept a safe distance when approaching the dam or returning from it.

The man watched us and we watched him, then one Saturday he gave us a passing 'Hello' that started a conversation and he invited us in. It was a typical Wearne two-bedroom fibro worker's cottage, the same as the piggery cottage of my childhood, which was only one kilometre away. Arthur Whitmarsh occupied one bedroom and Lordly the other. He had removed the door between Lordly's 'bedroom' and the kitchen area and inserted a barrier just high enough to impede the giant stallion from joining him at the small kitchen table, although I'm not sure Arthur would have minded if he had. Lordly, standing in his bedroom, would poke his head out and join the conversation. Once Arthur asked us to pretend to hit him, and Lordly put his ears back and tried to bite us.

Arthur and Lordly were at North Rocks taking advantage of the cottage and a steady flow of mares owned by Dr Wearne for his daughter Mary Lou, who was an accomplished equestrian. Arthur and Lordly had a wonderful relationship: Arthur collected the stud fees and Lordly had female variety. Arthur was only thirty years old in that spring of 1954 and the beautiful Lordly, a son of the great racehorse High Caste, was in his prime at just one year younger than me.

A couple of visits and we were at home with Arthur and Lordly. We made endless lunches of tinned spaghetti between white bread, toasted in a jaffle iron that fitted neatly into the firebox of the wood stove. There was no electricity, and Arthur would wind up a gramophone to play Kenny Gardner singing 'Tennessee Waltz' and Slim Whitman singing 'Rose Marie' over and over again. We worshipped Arthur, Lordly, the music, the jaffles and the acceptance. We were there every weekend, all weekend. Arthur had the occasional visit from a lady friend who we never met, and for those weekends he was not available to us.

Arthur took me with him when he checked out another location for Lordly's pleasant vocation in life at Cecil Park, which seemed way out in the country to me and probably was. There I saw my first flocks of white cockatoos among the remaining trees on the other side of the Cumberland Plain; from there they would eventually launch their assault on suburban Sydney.

When the breeding season was over and all the mares were pregnant, Arthur and Lordly left my life and I never saw him again. That is where it would have ended if there had not been one brief and obscure obituary on Arthur written by Brian Russell and published in the *Virtual Form Guide* of November 2007. I tracked down Brian to try to close the circle. He revealed that Arthur was widely and likeably known as the 'gypsy breeder' because he travelled with one of his stallions wherever there were enough mares for him to set up his caravan or rent a cottage. He took stallions to mares around the outer fringes of Sydney and as far away as Cowra. Arthur never married or had children and spent an inheritance and modest income on dressing and living well with his horses in Marion Street, Leichhardt in Sydney.

Lordly and three other stallions resided in stables known as 'boxes' in that Leichhardt backyard. There was only a very narrow passageway between Arthur's house and the house next door. The huge Lordly could walk along the passage, but when he died in his box, the only way Arthur's beloved stallion could be removed was to dismember him and load him in pieces onto a truck parked out the front in Marion Street.

Owning a roving stallion became less profitable as stud farms became more specialised in catering specifically to different sectors of the horse industry. Arthur later became a stalwart of Haberfield Rowing Club and helped prepare the rowing team for the 1988 Seoul Olympics. He smoked heavily and ultimately suffered a stroke that left him confined to a wheelchair, sharing his house in his last few years with another disabled man. I remember the gypsy breeder with great fondness for that brief time when he was young, and Lordly, Robbie and I were even younger.

~

At primary school I became friends with Andy Crosby. The Crosbys lived in a dairy in a small cottage they leased, in which they squeezed eight of their children. Mrs Crosby was as short and broad as Mr Crosby was lean and tall. She never spoke to me and I never got inside their house or was offered a drink or hospitality of any kind.

From down in my snicklegrub pit I was desperate for some kindness, but I could only glimpse a kitchen crowded with kids and pots. There were ten or so kids; Andy told me that once when the eldest girl came home to visit and he responded to her knock at the front, he told his mother there was a stranger at the door.

Near the dairy was a large, square, concrete-lined well that confined a spring coming out of the side of a hill. The well held fear and attraction in equal proportions. Andy liked to tell me that kittens from the many cats that patrolled the dairy ended their short lives there in a sack weighted with a brick. It was always out of bounds and the wire netting's physical barrier, close around its vertical concrete walls, was extended by an invisible but severely enforced 50-metre boundary we feared to cross but served to increase its mystique. Getting a closer look involved secrecy or an excuse such as going past it as close as possible when getting the cows in.

The cows were milked by hand as they dined on waste barley from Resch's Brewery. It was still steaming from fermentation as it was shovelled into the troughs but its smell, together with fresh cow shit that was kept moist by constant pissing, was not unpleasant.

Andy, like me, was conscripted to his father's life, but he loved the dairy and became a dairy farmer himself. He responded readily to my dare to eat fresh, sloppy, hot cow dung. Well, he didn't actually 'eat' it, but he certainly took a big taste. He and I were workers: he pulled cows' tits and I pulled wheelbarrows, and we grew fit and strong from it. He was growing tall and excelled in the high jump, while I was shorter and became the fastest sprinter in our school.

Andy and his brothers each had their own horse, which no one else was allowed to ride. This band of brothers, dressed in clean, neatly pressed western shirts and jeans topped by cowboy hats, rode up North Rocks Road one Sunday a month on their way to pony club. Andy wouldn't speak to me if I happened to be near when they rode past.

Robbie and I were probably pushing our latest billycart up the road or designing dams modelled out of clay in the bitumen-free gutter, ready for the next big rain. The Crosby brothers were royalty, and we were footmen. There were no teenage girls with ponies who might let me ride them now and then. There was no ladder to those good-looking Crosby boys so magnificently high on their horses.

Andy's father always frightened the shit out of me. He was tall, distant and half-angry at the best of times, and the lure of the dairy and all its animals was the only thing that could overcome my fear of him. He raced any animal attached to prize money; pigeons, greyhounds, trotters and gallopers all got a run. His enthusiasms waxed and waned, but sometimes more than one was in training. After all, he had all those kids who could feed and water the race animals and walk the greyhound contingent.

The world of horses, farms and bush might have happened much faster for me if only Andy Crosby and I had followed our sophisticated and detailed planning and run away. Andy, mounted on his horse and leading a spare saddled horse belonging to one of his brothers, was supposed to meet me after sundown. Under the cover of night we planned to get to Castle Hill, where the real country started. We would camp hidden in the bush during the next day and get to Windsor the next night, putting us beyond the reach of anyone who might search for us. Food, clothing and shelter were only minor requirements for a life without care on the open range.

Each time I would be ready and waiting at the appointed time with a small bag of clothes and some slices of white bread I had pilfered from the bread bin without being noticed. Secrecy was essential if we were to make our getaway before bedtime and before my parents discovered that their son, Roland the budding cowboy, was gone. There was only one minor hitch: Andy never turned up with the horses.

He always had an excuse at school the next day and we would set yet another plan, but of course Andy had much more skin in the game than me. Absconding, not only with his own horse but with one belonging to a brother, would have resulted in disastrous consequences at the hands of his tough father. In the end I had to satisfy my intense desire to ride horses via a different route.

I depended on the Billabong books by Mary Grant Bruce about the Linton family of Billabong Station, who celebrated the Australian bush values of hard work and mateship. I fell in love with the mustang Flicka in the three books by Mary O'Hara. I rode Black Beauty between the classic lines Anna Sewell had crafted. *Kings in Grass Castles* by Mary Durack told me to hasten lest I miss my calling. The cowboy and Indian films at the Saturday afternoon session at the Civic in Parramatta brought horses and cowboys alive. I could even forgive the cowboys for blasting the heads off rattlesnakes at fifty paces with a pistol shot from the hip because of their incredible speed and accuracy.

~

Andy and I went our separate ways after primary school, having been allocated to different high schools. In my second year at high, when I was still only thirteen, I became friends with Tommy Schweitzer. Tommy, by the way, was the first person I ever saw eating capsicums: his parents made him salami and capsicum sandwiches on lovely white Vienna loaf. I wanted Mum to make me white bread sandwiches with tomato sauce and peanut butter like the other kids, but she gave me schwarzbrot with liverwurst, which I ate out of sight behind my school case lid.

Tommy's parents had recently arrived from Hungary and had established a successful leathergoods business. Wanting the best Australia had to offer for their eldest son, they bought him a beautiful black gelding. However, Wizard came with such uptight equine tension that, once he was saddled, he broke into a foaming lather of sweat and jogged on the spot. A steady walk for a beginner was beyond him.

His parents sought the advice of Mr Crosby. I was at the assessment, sitting quietly nearby, when the Schweitzers must have mentioned my name, to which Mr Crosby said well within my earshot that 'Breckwoldt couldn't ride a rail'. I knew exactly what he meant: I could not even sit on a cow yard rail let alone ride a horse. Painful, hurtful, belittling in front of my friend and his parents and totally unnecessary.

The lizard part of me kept reading every Gerald Durrell book I could lay my hands on. On leaving school at the age of fourteen, I wrote to him at his famous zoo to ask for a job. Not realising I would be one of thousands doing the same, I was disappointed to receive the standard reply: thanks, but Mr Durrell is away on a collecting expedition and he will reply if an employment opportunity arises.

I then read an article in a magazine about a person who specialised in catching anacondas in the Amazon to supply zoos. I sent a letter to him asking for employment, but that went nowhere. My parents believed that becoming a jackeroo was the best option to fulfil the cowboy in me, but they were convinced it was impossible to be employed as a jackeroo before the age of seventeen.

Holm and Mum always found reasons against me getting a horse, even though I was prepared to finance the operation myself. I knew they were inexpensive because during the school holidays I had caught the bus to Parramatta and walked to the Friday horse sale. I watched the bidding and saw that most of the horses went to the knackery near Windsor to be turned into pet food. Ten pounds could buy a riding horse of reasonable looks.

A couple of kids I didn't know befriended me at one of those horse sales; they suggested we pool our funds to buy a horse we could share. I contributed two pounds and three shillings to the purchase. They disappeared shortly thereafter, along with my money. Scammed.

I took the initiative and asked Mr Schultz, the man who had ran over me in his Plymouth many years earlier, whether he would allow me to put a horse on a vacant paddock next to his house. He agreed, and that removed a major impediment. Mum got around that by saying there was too much grass in that paddock and the horse would die of bloat. To seal it, she added that my legs were not yet strong enough to squeeze the air out of a horse if its temperament or speed demanded immediate control.

Both incorrect, of course. Horses are not ruminants and do not bloat, although they can founder on good feed if not exercised. Anyhow that was no problem, because I was going to be on it every spare moment. Also, no human can squeeze the air out of a horse's lungs with the power of their legs when mounted. Whether she truly believed this was the case or plucked it randomly from a 'reasons not to get a horse' list I do not know.

Watching Mr Loder, the pound keeper, doing his monthly beat only made my longing for a horse even worse. He was a cross between Canadian mountie and a cowboy when he rode his big bay horse along North Rocks Road on his monthly beat. People whispered, 'Be careful or 'e'll pound yer dog', and his control over some distant animal prison added to his aura. Loder never spoke; he only rode by as if in another world. In which, indeed, he resided.

The Crosbys, Mr Loder, Bonnie the Clydesdale, the Taffy pony at Sanday's dairy, which was always for sale—they all got inside me and changed something without me knowing it. Up to then I had never seen any of the family photographs that included Holm in his First World War uniform mounted on his good-looking horse or of Holm and Mum in jodhpurs somewhere in Shanghai, so I doubt there were any early subliminal influences, but I cannot discount them either.

5

A JOB IN AGRICULTURE

I was meek and mild in class at primary school and boisterous
in the playground, where I was attracted to every contagious
activity. No sooner had marbles got boring than cigarette
packets took over, before swapping cicadas and hatching
silkworms from eggs stored in shoeboxes. Allow me one item
of self-aggrandisement because there is not much else I was
good at, other than being a speedy sprinter.

I had heard about Hurlstone Agricultural High School at
Glenfield and set my heart on going there without any idea of
how I would travel there and back each day, but that dream
never materialised. I was in bed and heard Mum and Holm
discussing that failure. It was curious that Holm was involved,
since he had never taken any interest in my education before
this. Clear as a bell I heard Mum say: 'The problem is he has
a low IQ.' That defined me for years.

I was assigned to Macquarie Boys High School, a notch
below the selective high schools but a notch above the local

technical high. However, my destination lost all lustre when I was relegated to 1C, where general maths, woodwork and technical drawing replaced the Latin, French and maths 1 and 2 taught to those in 1A. They were headed for university. You get the drift: I was one above the 'special' mob in 1D.

My performance in high school began so poorly that by the end of my first two terms I was demoted to 1D, right down there with those kids in the special class. Stuart Smith, who had been in the same class as me in primary school and was now in 1A, told me on the bus that he was studying at night and weekends for an exam. I honestly did not know what he was talking about: how would you go about such an activity, and why on earth would you do that at night and on a weekend? My demotion got Mum's attention and she got Angela to give me nightly coaching every day of the week, which got me back into 2C the following year. It seemed like an achievement. I can now reflect on my wasted school years and realise that I was totally unengaged throughout. School had no relevance to the life I led then or wanted in the future.

My one regret about high school is that I did not play any sport. Wednesday afternoon sport was compulsory, but I developed a neat way of avoiding it. I would enrol for cricket and then, too late for any crosschecking, I would cancel that and say I was going to soccer. Safely off any roll, I would walk to Parramatta with a couple of other rogues along the stormwater drain. We lit bunches of newspaper to find our long way through tunnelled sections—how dumb was that?—to avoid being seen near the school bus stop. Then I would go and swim in Lake Parramatta and get my exercise as a loner.

Despite the good efforts of some memorable teachers, I left Macquarie Boys High at the age of fourteen and nine months with a bare pass in four subjects, but enough for an intermediate certificate. Free at last, I vowed to never, ever set foot in an educational institution again. Weekday imprisonment was finally over.

~

Holm came up with a plan to get me close to agriculture. He was a works architect at the University of Sydney and asked fellow German Professor Breyer, professor of agricultural chemistry, whether there might be an opportunity for me in the Faculty of Agriculture. Professor Breyer immediately employed me as a laboratory technician in training without an application or interview. Holm and Mum must have been relieved that their son of limited intelligence got a good job.

There had been no discussions about alternatives, with something like: 'Well, son, it looks like academia is not your forte. But you are really good with animals, so why don't we think about a career as a zookeeper?' It did not cross their minds, or they did not fancy the idea that their son might have a career shovelling elephant dung. Come to think about it, being a zookeeper would have been an attractive option.

Young and malleable, I took on being a laboratory technician in training with enthusiasm. To become a fully-fledged laboratory technician involved a four-year technical course that I was not qualified to enter because I had failed in general mathematics and chemistry in the intermediate certificate, so in just a matter of months I broke my vows and went to

Meadowbank Technical College two nights a week to repeat maths and chemistry.

My job was not without some pleasures. I became friends with handsome Tony Potts, who came from Bondi and seemed so cool compared to me, the awkward Westie. I admired the way he looked and dressed, and modelled myself on him with limited success. We would go to the gym together at lunchtime and do a lot of big talk.

Holm worked close by and occasionally took me out to dinner, followed by a show at the Tivoli Theatre. I wonder how much those nights were for me and how much they were for him. I was embarrassed when he finished his plate and would immediately deposit it on the nearest clean vacant table so he didn't have to look at it. Then it was off to the Tivoli, where long-legged, statuesque, bare-breasted show-girls stood behind the entertainers.

The showgirls were naked from the waist up; the laws at that time insisted they were not allowed to move. There was very little below their waist to separate those bare breasts from their bare long legs. Holm would take out his opera glasses and focus them on the showgirls from curtain up to curtain down as I sank low in my seat and was not there. I would remain surly and silent on the train to Parramatta, and in the taxi from there to home.

My work colleagues prepared me for the more important things in life, such as how to mix pure alcohol with Fanta in the lab's big jars. I demonstrated my excellent rock-throwing ability when I threw glass jars left behind by students on their benches to the front, where Bernie Brightman, a couple of years my senior, caught them in a cardboard box so they could be returned to their cupboard.

I was truly gifted at this important professional role, but I once threw too fast for Bernie to catch and hit him on the forehead with a jar thrown over the benches from the back of the lab. He fell unconscious, but I had kept my first aid meticulously up to date so I quickly filled a wooden tray—meant for the time-wasting and boring task of actually collecting the jars from the benches—with water and tipped it over him. He revived, and we got on with the job of throwing and catching jars.

The best part was going to the Homebush Abattoirs to collect pancreas, kidney and liver offcuts for student experiments on enzymes. I liked going there and seeing the cattle milling in the slaughter yards, even though they were doomed. The laboratory work preparing their offal did involve some expertise, and once when other people were on leave I had to do this alone. I was highly commended for my work by the staff and by Professor Breyer.

This became my life and I could not see it changing, but in January 1960 there came a letter from my half-brother, Helmut.

~

Helmut, Holm's son from his first marriage, had arrived in Australia in 1951 on the assisted passage scheme. Helping Germans getting here so soon after the war was an irony lost in the mantra of 'populate or perish', an insecurity that fed an obsessional dependence on Great Britain, but there were not enough 'ten-pound Poms' to fill the demand. The Immigration Restriction Act 1901 (the White Australia policy) had been enacted to protect the goldfields from an invasion of Chinese competitors and was not entirely dismantled until 1966. Without enough 'good' white people available, in 1949 the Menzies government opened the gate for 'appropriate' Northern Europeans. West Germany got the nod in late 1951 and Helmut came in the first wave; he was bonded to a German construction company contracted to build prefabricated housing commission homes in Cowra.

Helmut's decision to come to Australia completed the circle of loss and family, although there was no inkling of it in our home. Holm never expressed any guilt or sense of loss over that earlier part of his life with another wife and two children, and we knew nothing of it. Helmut was only seven when Holm left him and his two-year-old sister, Geisa, for a new wife in a new country to start a new family. Holm had subsequently written to his ex-wife describing the wonderful opportunities in China, and then Australia, for Helmut.

The imminent arrival of an instant older brother had me totally enraptured. I was seven years old when we caught the train to Wynyard and walked down to Circular Quay. Passengers from the Lloyd Triestino Line's huge, sparkling new *Neptunia*, which had departed from Bremerhaven, were disembarking down the gangplanks just as we got there.

No customs officers, no barriers, no sniffer dogs: nothing impeded the spill of humanity from that ship. Germans, Italians, Poles, Yugoslavs, Lithuanians, Greek, soon to be neatly bundled under the 'New Australian' label as krauts, dagos, wogs and Slavs.

I held tightly to one of Mum's hands while Holm cupped his hands to trumpet 'Helmut!', and from barely a few steps away there was a reply, and I had a new big brother aged twenty-seven. I wanted to show Helmut everything. I could throw rocks, make a catapult, set traps for sparrows made of bricks with paddle pop sticks as triggers and catch lizards of all sizes and I knew the way to and from the bush and all its hidden little secrets, such as the old convict road. I wanted his time so I could show him all this magic, and he lapped it up.

Helmut had been conscripted at the age of eighteen and sent to the Russian front. Fortunately, an almost completed apprenticeship as an architectural draughtsman resulted in him being deployed behind the lines to draft maps and design protective concrete bunkers. His mother had advanced tuberculosis and spent the war in a sanatorium; both she and Geisa survived, but food in post-war Germany was scarce.

North Rocks Primary School had just got a big new classroom, built to accommodate the consequences of the rapid post-war breeding in our expanding community. Helmut offered to paint a huge mural on the wall behind where the teacher stood in the main classroom. He chose an Australian scene of a gum tree and Aboriginal man with spear and boomerang and signed it Helmut Breckwoldt. There I would sit in a classroom with his painting to look at and his signature for all to see, his surname the same as mine. His mural was a celebration of Australia from someone just arrived.

The prefabricated houses for Cowra were a disaster. All neatly cut to size in Germany, they did not comply with Australian standards. Helmut was immediately redeployed to building the new power station at Wallerawang, near Lithgow.

And then Helmut was gone. No explanation; nothing said. My big brother disappeared, and no reason was provided to me. I would certainly have asked, but I was not told. Nothing was said of the big brother who had come with such promise and then disappeared.

~

It had been eight years since Helmut had vanished and Holm must have been relieved to hear from him because he showed me the letter, which was unusual for him. Helmut now lived in Monto in the Central Highlands of Queensland with his wife, Gwen, the daughter of a dairy farmer, and two children. He was a builder and they owned a corner store that was attached to their home and managed by Gwen. He mentioned, just as an item of news, that one of his recent projects had been building a homestead on a cattle station.

My decision was instant and utterly resolute: I wrote to Helmut that night and informed him I was coming to join him, to get a job on a cattle station.

Our home use of the newly acquired telephone was parsimonious and it had not yet replaced handwritten correspondence. More importantly, I needed to avoid any 'sensible' conversations between him and my parents that might interfere with my immediate travel plans. Similarly, I did not ask Helmut if it was appropriate; that might also get in my way.

It is, of course, possible that Holm and Mum were relieved at my decision to stay with Helmut, who could parachute me into, or gently out of, the life of being a cowboy.

Professor Breyer called me to his office to counsel me against such a foolhardy move. He said I would find my new life unbearably cruel, and the men so rough and tough that I would not cope. But the good professor sensed my determination, hidden under my awkward shyness, and said that if I did not find it to my liking he would always give me my old job back. I was touched, and probably mumbled a thank you. It was one of the few times in that early part of my life that I felt valued. Angela was now married and living another life. I cannot recall saying goodbye to her or my young brother, Chris, who had been born nine years earlier. Sadly, any farewells would have been cursory because I was so excited at leaving home.

On the day I left home, Mum drove Holm and me to Granville Station in her car, where we caught a train to Central Station. I had all my belongings in a fake crocodile-skin overnight bag and also carried a big, brand new .303/25 in a loose plastic rifle carry bag.

As the train was about to depart Granville Station, Holm turned to me and said: 'Make sure you wave goodbye to your mother.' That was the first and only time I ever experienced him being concerned about Mum's feelings. I turned and waved goodbye without the poignancy I now feel for the event.

I was a month short of sixteen and on an adventure; I was incredibly happy to be leaving home. I wonder, but will never know, what Holm and Mum were feeling. I can tear up about it now but, like so many things in my life, too late.

6

GO NORTH,
YOUNG MAN

Seated in second class on the train from Central to Brisbane, I got talking to the older man sitting next to me. Our train arrived in Brisbane late in the evening. When he heard that my train for Monto did not leave until the next morning and that I had not worked out where to stay overnight, he asked me whether I would like to share his hotel room. I happily accepted his offer without even considering any ulterior motives or consequences. Clearly the budgerigar incident had not had any lasting effect.

This man was simply a concerned and helpful person; maybe it was he who was taking the risk with this kid carrying a big rifle. He kindly arranged for the hotel staff to put a mattress on the floor of his room and I slept there soundly and comfortably, but I worry now that I did not thank him properly. This is a troubling constant theme in my life: did I thank people enough? I am sure that residual guilt about my mother's distressful fits of woe left me with feelings that I do not do or say enough when I could or should.

The rail trip from Brisbane to Monto revealed a wonderment of different bush and farms. There were dry, open forests of ironbark over kangaroo grass and large irrigated citrus orchards on the Lower Burnett. The train stopped at the cattle town of Eidsvold, 430 kilometres from Brisbane and one stop before Monto. Here Helmut boarded the train and searched through the carriages to find me. He and his building crew were camped there during the week while they were building a church. The budding cowboy became an instant builder's labourer.

Helmut arranged an introduction for me with Barney Joyce, the highly respected owner of Eidsvold Station and probably a patron of the new church. Joyce was instrumental in breeding and promoting Santa Gertrudis cattle, only recently imported from the United States. In moleskin trousers, brown corduroy coat and a town cattleman's hat with its brim slightly curled, he seemed all powerful. Although we were of a similar height, he towered over me with his aura. His square stance and confidence proclaimed that the town, and everything beyond it, belonged to him. My hesitant mumbling meant our interview was over in moments. Joyce did not see much potential in the inarticulate and unimpressive-looking builder's labourer in shorts and sandshoes.

Even if Joyce had had no vacancy for me he had a wide network of station owners who might have taken on a beginner, but I gave him permission to kill that stone dead right there in that moment of all my enthusiasm. There was nothing stopping me suggesting I could do voluntary work while he assessed my ability. I could have asked him for some career advice or inquired if some other station owners would give me a start, but I was devoid of social skills and just stood there without giving him a glimpse of who I might be or become. Although I never met Barney Joyce again, there would be another connection with him only two years into the future.

My first introduction to a cattle baron failed, but Monto was kind to me. It services a mixed farming district, with dairies and piggeries amid crops of sorghum and maize. There were enough larger cattle properties in and around Monto to give me hope, even if it had stalled after that one setback. I liked Gwen very much and felt at home.

Helmut took me on a trip to Fraser Island, along with a new canoe he had built. At Hervey Bay we commissioned the owner of a fishing boat to take us out to the island and drop us off at a remote spot near a ruined wharf. Helmut had fashioned an outrigger for his canoe, and I tried to spearfish from it. We camped next to a small freshwater stream so we had drinking water. Out of fear of sharks, we only ever bathed in shallow sea water and never swam in the ocean. I climbed out on the old wharf and caught whiting for breakfast, lunch and dinner. Helmut took his German shepherd, Prince, along and tethered him at night. Dingoes came right into our camp to attack this intruder and we would frighten them away with shouts and banging of the billy can. Fraser Island was devoid of tourists then and we revelled in its wilderness. It was during this trip that Helmut told me that the long rift with Holm had been about money. Helmut had obtained some waste building materials that Holm wanted and had them delivered by a commercial courier who Holm refused to pay. Totally believable.

Helmut introduced me to a firm of stock and station agents in Monto and I accompanied them to the weekly cattle sale. I jealously watched a father and son bring their cattle in on horseback and draft them into lots ready for auction. I envied their looks, clothes and confidence and the way the father and son worked together. My enthusiasm must have crept out of its cage, because when I attended more sales the manager of the stock and station agency asked if I would like to join their company as a trainee auctioneer. You know the theme by now: I might not have thanked him enough, but my heart was still firmly set on working on a cattle station.

That opportunity arose soon thereafter from a person very different from Barney Joyce, although no less successful. Ken Rawlinson was a small, wiry moneylender and insurance broker; his thriftiness was demonstrated by his habit of travelling around town on a bicycle while dressed in a shirt, shorts and sandals. His reputation of being the wealthiest person in Monto was, no doubt, confirmed by his family living in a two-storey brick house with a swimming pool, not a common thing in Monto in 1960.

Ken came to Gwen's shop to assess its annual insurance requirements and I happened to be there. After Gwen explained my presence in Monto, Ken turned to me and said,

'Well, if you want a job on a cattle station, you should go and talk to Sam Nugent.'

Go and talk to Sam Nugent I did. He worked in a butcher's shop in Monto, but he had once been the overseer on a large cattle station in the Gulf of Carpentaria called Augustus Downs. He'd left there in the most tragic circumstances after his eighteen-year-old son Leon had been killed in a horse accident.

Sam said he would write to the manager of Augustus Downs and recommend me for a job as a ringer, which was the first time I heard a word that would become so familiar to me. It took about fifty years before I connected the dots and worked out that I got a job on a cattle station as the result of a horse fatality.

Just a week later I received a telegram via the Royal Flying Doctor Service from Reg Nissen, the manager of Augustus Downs: 'We can give you a start. You will need a six foot by four foot piece of canvas and blankets. If you stay for three months we will refund your fare. You will need to fly TAA out of Cloncurry and advise me your date of arrival.'

Gwen wrote to my mother on 9 March 1960, not long after Sam Nugent's intervention:

I must begin with an apology of not writing earlier, I wanted to write immediately on Roland's arrival, to tell you how pleased we are to have him with us, and to thank you most sincerely for the exquisite clothes you have sent for the children, but (perhaps Roland has told you). The shop keeps me busy from 7.30am to 9.00pm, so with the babies I don't have much spare time. Roland proves his adaptability by fitting in uncomplainingly to quite a hectic schedule.

We are delighted with Roland, he is a fine boy and makes a favorable impression on all whom he meets. Already he has a friend his own age (who has a car & an influential father), and I think there are several young ladies who would like to be his friend. But he has a poor opinion of Q'ld girls & still thinks blissfully of the ones he left behind.

I hope Roland does not find a job for a while—it is good not to be living by myself while Helmut is away. He is quite versatile and has done everything from feeding the baby to a full-scale ant extermination campaign.

He has applied for a job on Augustus Downs, at Cloncurry 1,500 miles from here. The conditions of work, & the future prospects are ideal, but oh, so far from home! He does seem too young to be really by himself in the world; but is remarkably self-reliant for his age & has a lot of determination, and in the cattle business, where one must begin from the very lowest, youth is an advantage.

Gwen probably got the idea that I was unenthusiastic about Queensland girls because of her failed attempts to pair me up with one of her shop assistants. If I gave any impression there were any girls I thought of back home it was to mask their non-existence.

I was a sixteen-year-old virgin and, based on my past experience (I mean the lack thereof) and my destination, it was highly likely I would retain that unenviable status for some time. My one and only love did not proceed beyond blissful kisses and ended suddenly after some months when she left a note in our mailbox saying it was all over. Mum had drawn my attention to the arrival of that note so she would have read it, but I said not a word about it and tried to bury the pain. I was good at that.

My first letter home was dated 22 March 1960 and it included: 'Dear Mum, I have got myself a job up north of Queensland on the second largest cattle station in Australia. The place is called Augustus Downs Station and it is 70 miles north of Cloncurry right in the Gulf country. The wages are eight pounds and ten shillings a week and board is free so I should have plenty of money. I will start work in Mid-April.'

I had exaggerated that Augustus Downs was the second largest cattle station in Australia, and how I arrived at that definition is beyond me. Put it down to exuberance. At 3107 square kilometres Augustus Downs is big, but it is a long way from the biggest, which is Anna Creek Station in South Australia at 24,446 square kilometres, about the size of Israel. The largest number of cattle on any one property is usually attributed to Brunette Downs on the Northern Territory Barkly Tableland, which runs up to 100,000 head on its 12,212 square kilometres.

The second significant item in the letter to my mother is that I refer to Holm as 'Dad'; I had started using that word again as a greeting when I wrote to him. I still wanted a dad and got one, whether he liked it or not, from the safety of distance.

~

Helmut, Gwen, Sam and Mrs Nugent saw me off at Monto for the train that would take me to Maryborough before heading north. Sam handed me a Hookey game, saying it had belonged to Leon and he would like me to hang it in the ringers' quarters in memory of his son. Leon had loved playing Hookey with the ringers on Augustus Downs and Sam hoped the current ringers would enjoy using it. It is a game in which small rubber quoits are thrown over hooks with a score under them, which are mounted on a backing piece the size of a dartboard. Sam and Mrs Nugent looked both sad and happy when seeing me off; I might have reminded them of their lost young son. I do not know why I never wrote to them.

Heading north on the Sunlander, I imagined myself mustering the clean white Brahman cattle that merged into the pale salt marsh country near St Lawrence north of Rockhampton. I arrived at Townsville station early next morning and left my luggage and rifle at the cloakroom to catch a ferry to explore Magnetic Island. I was totally alone but did not feel it.

Late that afternoon I boarded the Inlander heading west. It crossed the Great Dividing Range in the dark and stopped at Charters Towers when it was in bed, with streetlights half-revealing buildings that kept the gold rush alive. In earlier times the people of Charters Towers had called it 'the world' because it had everything you could ever want with its theatres and thriving commerce, including its own stock exchange. Now it was a service town for cattle stations and the government, with boarding schools of different denominations casting their nets to catch students across the West and on the Gulf, up to Cape York and Torres Strait.

The town's unchanged railway station and our night rattle through its dimmed lights confirmed to me that this was the entry point to my frontier. I had a warm rush of emotion, like falling in love.

Hours later the light of dawn told me I was well inside that frontier and on the black-soil downs somewhere between Richmond and Hughenden. Not long afterwards there were hazy lines of gutta-percha and gidgee in the distance, above a mirage of a shimmering inland sea created by the heat-fractured morning air. I filled that huge open space with exhilarating possibilities that had me at the centre of each one.

There were sheep and cattle and large bustards or plains turkey, all in easy sight of the train window. Julia Creek came and passed before the sheep became fewer and the trees became denser as the Mitchell and Flinders grasses of the downs gave way to the stony hills around Cloncurry.

That long train journey had happened in an instant and I now alighted at Cloncurry, a small railway and mining town that serviced cattle stations, including those in the Gulf of Carpentaria. This time I had the wit to get a hotel room.

Reg Nissen had booked me a seat next day on the early morning Gulf run of the lumbering TAA DC-3, that reliable carthorse of the outback sky. From Cloncurry the Gulf run served cattle stations as well as the small agglomeration of houses and pub at Gregory, the missions at Mornington Island and Doomadgee, then on to Burketown and back to Cloncurry via Normanton.

Not long out of Cloncurry, the rocky hills and silver broad-leaved eucalypts gave way to patches of grassland before our first landing at Granada Station, its red roofs and neat white buildings confirming my image of what a remote cattle station should look like. It was a friendly oasis that wanted to be there. Green lawns surrounded a large station manager's house, with the rest of the buildings in a neat grid pattern as though forming a small town.

The roof of the big shed near the cattle yards had 'Granada' painted on it in big white letters, a territorial marker as well as convenient identification for the only other aerial visitor in those years before the Cessna traffic arrived: the flying doctor. Granada was owned by the Australian Estates Company Limited, a big English pastoral company that had taken over the debts incurred by its previous Melbourne-based owners. I was convinced that Augustus Downs would look the same as Granada, if not better.

There was something else about Granada. The attractive young hostess, as they were called then, took the vacant seat beside me for the landing and asked if I was going to Augustus Downs to be a cowboy, whereupon I informed her, with some authority, that I was going to be a ringer.

Sam Nugent had explained to me that in Australia cowboys milked the station cows and/or goats for the manager and family, as well as tended the vegetable patch and did odd jobs. 'Ringer' was the title given to stockmen, and the name derived from galloping to the front of a mob of fractious cattle and circling them around to slow them down.

After our take-off from Granada, the friendly young hostess started her refreshments round. When she came to my seat, she asked me whether I preferred 'coffee, tea or me?'.

I was so unbelievably slow when it came to women that it only dawned on me three days later that the 'me' option would have been more interesting than the tea I chose.

There was no chance of joining the mile-high club anyway. We were now flying low above the grassed downs and scattered trees, ready for landing at Kamilaroi, then Lorraine Station, before my final destination of Augustus Downs.

7

ARRIVAL

My silver bird circled the red-gravelled strip to make sure it was clear of straying cattle. It taxied in with twin propellers pulling red dust over itself as a repaint to match the claypan. Reg Nissen was there to collect me and to swap incoming for outgoing mail.

I became transfixed by his hat as he chatted with the pilots. Years of sweat had painted jagged mountains above his plaited kangaroo-hide hatband, which circled a huge Akubra Stetson. A sloping fold ran from its peak to a brim that was curled at its leading edges, enough to say 'cattleman' without reducing shade. There was nothing casual about it; it had been shaped and reshaped every time it was picked up then forged by wind and sun. My army disposal hat lay crushed inside my fake crocodile-skin overnight bag.

Reg was of average height, with a bend to him. Not stooped, just a curve acquired by a lifetime of work on a cattle station. His hat shaded clear eyes set in an open, smiling face. He had been managing Augustus Downs for more than thirty years, long enough for respect to replace authority. Some called him 'Boss' while others called him 'Mr Nissen'. I stuck to my well-worn path of not calling him anything. Reg liked to laugh at his little jokes and described station work as 'easy as shitting in bed and kicking it out with your feet'. Lurking within that job description were multiple performance criteria, many of them not that easy to achieve.

Driving from the air strip to the station—no one called them *homesteads* in the north—Reg made no comment about my .303/25 rifle. Most ringers had a rifle knocking about unprotected in the backs of trucks and the boots of cars; whereas pets such as cats or dogs were out of the question, a rifle was neither here nor there. They were useful for shooting brumbies, although that was not my intention so early in the piece. I was after the exotic without any clear idea of what form that would take; maybe a buffalo?

Hoping to be eased out of my insecurity, I asked Reg what the head stockman was like. 'Pretty useless,' came the instant reply. Shaken by such frankness and insecure enough already, I was too shy to inquire into the head stockman's inadequacy. There was no human resource management department here to gently induct the recruit and cloak a raw human response with appropriate corporate tact.

The station itself was raw, so perhaps his reply reflected a pervasive approach to life. No outback oasis to greet me here. The station buildings sat on red soil from which any low eucalypts had been cleared. They were located just far enough from the Leichhardt River to avoid most floods, but close enough for the diesel pump to deliver its muddy water. Unpainted corrugated-iron buildings were connected to the red soil by a patina of dust.

The manager's house was occupied by Reg and Mrs Nissen, who I never spoke to and rarely saw. It was of pole construction, with small-windowed rooms upstairs and a wide, gauzed-in breezeway underneath that provided relief from the heat for the kitchen and eating areas. No sprawling gardens, no expansive lawns around the boss's 'big house'; just a tight fence to protect a small vegetable garden from the station goat herd.

Behind that was a tin shed known as the 'store', and 50 metres across from that were the ringers' quarters. Our showers and toilet were in a separate building near our back stairs, as was the laundry with its copper. Beyond our quarters were the cook's quarters, with its kitchen and a small dining room with a wooden table and bench seating. A good 100 metres away, down near the horse yards, stood about five small one-roomed tin sheds on concrete slabs; these housed the Aboriginal ringers.

Kidman Brody Company did not regard architecture or landscape design as an investment, so pragmatism ruled and nothing escaped the money razor. There was no chance of image displacing function; here was basic shelter for the workers. Surveying all this the first time, my dream was badly dented, but I soon switched to recovery mode and waited for the ringers to arrive back from mustering the Steer Paddock.

The first to greet me was Jack McGynn, the 'useless' head stockman. His first words to me were, 'Do you smoke?'

I hesitated, looked at the floor and mumbled. Too slow. 'Here: this will last you until the store opens on Saturday morning,' as he kindly handed me a packet of tobacco and papers from his supply. Apart from the tightly rolled newspaper in the double-decker cave with Robbie and graduating to dried cow dung with Andy, I had only smoked one cigarette and that had left me violently ill and vomiting. I hid all that, so badly did I want to fit in, and I took the offered packet of tobacco and papers.

I had excellent role models in learning how to smoke. Hang a paper on your bottom lip while carefully kneading the exact amount of tobacco between finger and palm. Take paper from lip and roll that finished product to a perfectly shaped cigarette. Not too fat. Not too thin. Delay gratification, holding it between your lips while slowly taking a match from a tin of Bell's Waterproof Wax Vestas matches held in its pouch on your belt. Strike it on the stippled underside of the tin. Light cigarette behind cupped hand as breeze protection. Take a long, relaxed first draw, its end glowing strongly, as if to say that all is well with the world. And that is the how I started smoking.

Jack McGinn was tall and topped by an angular face with deep-set eyes at the end of his long nose above a well-clipped moustache. To me he looked the real deal, with blue-grey moleskin trousers tucked into leggings above Cuban-heeled R.M. Williams boots. I could see no reason why Reg described him as incompetent; then again, being totally incompetent myself, I had no ruler by which to measure him.

It was explained to me later that Reg's disdain for Jack arose only a short time after he was appointed, when he was introduced to his team of horses. Angel was one of the head stockman's team and had been ridden by Les Cockerill, the previous head stockman. Reg mentioned that Angel could really buck and was difficult to stay on if she put her mind to it. Apparently, Jack immediately allocated her to one of the other ringers instead of taking her on himself.

Jack had taken up horse riding too late in life to ride tough horses and to set an example to the others. Part of that 'easy as shit' thing was that a head stockman should never allocate a horse to another ringer that he (it was all *he* then) would not ride himself. Despite that limitation, Jack was strong and tough enough, having been a commando in the Korean War. I regret not asking him what he did during that forgotten war, and how he got there and back alive. I had landed inside a cultural fence, as strong as the real thing; it held in our feelings, insecurities, hopes and dreams. Its strength lay in its unspoken rule: 'Don't probe too much. I'll tell you everything you need to know if I feel like it.'

That was the wire, and we were the posts standing separately along it: connected, important, yet replaceable. The upside was that I was not asked about 'Breckwoldt'. No tiresome, 'Oh, that sounds Dutch, or is it German or Polish or something?' Nothing about my past, nothing at all, not even how I got to Augustus Downs in the Gulf of Carpentaria from Sydney in 1960 at the tender age of sixteen. I had landed in an emotional safety zone and I now ponder whether that was part of my journey.

I had been on the outside looking in for as long as I could remember. So powerful was this effect that it meant never feeling comfortable or that I belonged, wholly or partly, but my father's marching to a different drummer credo had given me resilience. Here at Augustus—as the newest, the youngest, the most inexperienced—I could rely on my ability not to give anything away and gladly relax into not being asked.

My professionalism at hiding my feelings was equalled by my capacity for profanity. Ralph Tate, one of my fellow ringers, told me later that I swore a lot in those first few days, which means I must have really sworn a lot for seasoned ringers to notice. I wanted to be part of the tribe and this was my feeble attempt to gain entry, deploying the only skill I could demonstrate at the time.

Yet they were quietly friendly to me in those first few days. Not an isolating quietude, but everyone gave each other space. Acceptance never articulated, but more closely confined than we realised or acknowledged. A small group of men in that vastness, we had to work, eat and sleep in a close-knit cattle camp day in and day out without a break. We all had baggage, but leaving it unopened was part of the deal.

Most of the year we spent at various established cattle camps, but when we were at the station we slept along each side of the breezeway in the ringers' quarters on metal folding beds carrying a fibre-filled mattress set on wire mesh. Two of us shared a room to the side of the wide breezeway to store our belongings.

Sandy, the short, powerfully built forty-five-year-old brightly blond Swedish sailor who was spending time on shore as the station cowboy, was the only person who slept in his room. Sandy wore a blue singlet, shorts and sandshoes;

he was meticulously clean and neat, habituated from his life as a sailor. He kept to himself and conferred only during one of his broad Swedish 'Holy dooley day' moments, such as when it had been a long walk to get the house cow in.

Keeping others awake by reading paperback westerns was solved by the background thump-thump of the station diesel generator being turned off promptly at eight every night. Kidman Brody saved diesel, as well as making sure we slept for a dawn start.

~

Folklore has it that the new chum is duped into mounting the station buckjumper to entertain the old hands. If any intent was present, then one look at me and the idea would have been quickly shelved. My inexperience was apparent in every tentative move I made approaching the horse in the round yard that had been drafted off for me on my first day of mustering; I could not even catch, bridle and saddle it. I was helped through those blurred minutes by Jack, who was patient enough without any time-wasting tutorial.

This was an oral world. The voice passed down knowledge about working horses that had accumulated over the ages across the world of the horse. No matter what task the horse faced—whether pulling a plough, a horse taxi or a coach in hand—you learned on the job by being told what to do and exactly how to do it.

Of course there were glorious exceptions, such as Xenophon, the Greek philosopher and soldier who lived from 430 to 350 BCE who is credited with writing the first manual on the correct use of the horse. He is oft quoted today with his 'everything that is forced cannot be beautiful' statement on working with horses. And there were the great academies of Europe, where dressage was part of a fully rounded education. Sophisticated manuals might not have reached the Gulf of Carpentaria, but the principles had. A clearly defined way of using station horses was embedded in what I was being taught, and it was precise and strict. I was being inducted into the world of the horse, from which I would never leave.

From the very start, I craved to be one of the station ringers and a horseman of note among them. I did not realise it then but I had two great advantages: I was young, and I was a clean slate without bad habits to unlearn.

The smell of leather, horse sweat and saddle grease, all perfumed into one, welcomed me into the saddle shed. I was allocated my own saddle and bridle, which I used for the next two years. My saddle had a saddlebag, curiously called a 'saddle pooch', on the near side and a quartpot in its pooch on the far side. It had small kneepads and a shallow dip, resulting in me learning to balance in a bucking session rather than rely on long kneepads and a deep dip. I should have bought it and kept it to this day. It did not take me long to learn from the others that being a good horseman relied on balance. Those who gripped with their legs had limited time in the saddle under a horse that had any ability to buck.

Nothing about learning to ride was easy. 'Do you want to get yourself fucking well killed?' made it clear that safety was an issue. This had nothing whatsoever to do with occupational health and safety, because the concept was non-existent. An accident on a distant cattle camp was both dangerous and a major disruption, and a long way from help. Was it avoiding an accident so that the day would not be disrupted, or was it looking out for others? Did it add up to the same thing? There was also an etiquette: when one person got off their horse to open a gate or have a drink at a waterhole, everyone would stop their horse and wait until he remounted and was ready to move off. If they kept on riding the person who'd dismounted could have difficulty remounting a horse that was trying to get back to its mates heading off.

It is easy to see how Aboriginal people at first contact thought rider and horse were one. The ringers were relaxed but taut in the saddle. The Australian stockman style was a blend of formal cavalry with the evolution of fit for purpose, to arrive at a controlled flexibility to meet the conditions of the bush. No one slouched in the saddle. Hands were always neat above the pommel and there were no 'chicken wings' in a canter or gallop.

Long, split reins without knots or buckles to connect them were universal. They could be used to flick a horse into a fast walk, then gathered up if there was need for a sudden burst of speed and a sharp turn with terrain changing under you and your horse. Jumping a log or quickly standing high in the stirrups meant leaning over your horse to get the weight off its hind legs in a flat-out gallop.

~

Even with three hundred working horses on Augustus it was difficult to find some that were quiet enough for a beginner, but after all those years of just wanting a horse I now became the proud owner of a team of horses. We each had a 'team' or 'string' and the better riders had up to fifteen or more horses each; over the next two years I would accumulate the same. No one else rode another ringer's horse unless it had been agreed to by him beforehand.

Out of those three hundred horses they managed to draft off four horses docile enough for a beginner such as me. Donkey was aptly named for his heavy body and short spiky mane, which never grew to compensate for his lack of other aesthetic attributes. Under saddle he was quiet, but once I got on him bareback and he threw me in seconds. Donkey had a thing about being ridden bareback and he threw those who tried it after I told them about his hang-up.

Strawberry had once been a beautiful strawberry roan gelding; now he was speckled with the long white hair of age and so thin that when I rode him I was on a skeleton held together by skin. Called up from the pension, he was hard to get going regardless of my urging. He had more up his sleeve, however, and one day he would show me what resources he could call upon if given the right incentive.

Fly was a pretty bay mare in the prime of her life. She was easy to saddle and mount, but she would literally fly once she got going and it took me a long time to develop the strength and capacity to hold her. Mum's advice about controlling wayward horses by squeezing the air out of their lungs with your legs did not work on Fly, and no one suggested this was a useful skill to acquire.

Laura was a beautiful brown mare who I liked to ride;

I would gaze at our combined shadow and marvel at how devastatingly lovely we looked together. Partly true, that is also an old station joke. With no one else to admire us, no large mirrors at the station or cattle camp, we had only our shadows. If someone got a bit too smart, another might respond with: 'Been looking at your shadow a bit too much lately?'

My first ride involved mustering the 155-square-kilometre Steer Paddock, which was next to the station complex. It housed the only set of big yards with a plunge dip and crush for any work that needed doing on the steers before they took one step closer to steak in the Bullock Paddock of the same size next door. The Steer Paddock was a mix of Mitchell and Flinders grasslands interspersed with a low open forest of broad-leaved eucalypts amid dense lines of gidgee acacia before running into the breakaways, the local name for the deep erosion gullies that could stretch out for a good kilometre either side of the river. The experienced ringers negotiated all that country at speed.

The steers were young and quick. They were not handled very often and probably held memories of a hot brand and sharp knife that had changed their future from grandly muscled bull to fattening eunuch. I was on Fly and struggled to keep up with the others the first morning. When we had a mob of about 300 steers together, I took up a quieter position on the tail to get familiar with my reins and saddle. That went well until one of the steers made a dash for freedom, accompanied by shouts of 'Bore him, Roly!' and 'Get round him, Roly!' and 'Quick, Roly!'.

Apparently, this was my golden opportunity to demonstrate the amazing horsemanship I had acquired during my
first morning on a horse. With those enthusiastic shouts of
encouragement, all eyes upon me and the steer about to
disappear into the timber, I took off in hot pursuit.

Fly must have been listening in because she demonstrated
the same commitment the ringers envisaged for me. She hit
full speed in a few strides and there was nothing I could do
to slow or guide her. Fly decided to go her side of a tree
instead of the side I thought we were committed to. My knee
connected with the tree at full gallop and I hit the ground
with a painful knee and no horse.

Fly then demonstrated that she did not need me at all,
galloping on at full speed with swinging empty stirrups. But,
like me, she did not have a clue what she was doing. Someone
galloped after her and brought her back, while another ringer
returned the wayward steer. I remounted, the all-round
excitement obliterating the pain from my knee. Amid great
laughter and recognition of my having a go, I was sincerely
advised that it would take another six busters before I could
make any claim to being a horseman.

Any accident or misadventure that did not result in a major
delay or injury would fill the evening space with laughter
and numerous versions in the retelling, until replaced by
another such event. It was the way intimacy was kept at bay.
Among the banter I did learn a critical lesson: there was no
place for the blame game. It started with horsemanship and
reached out from there to every aspect of station life.

If you came off your horse you never blamed the horse. It

might be a difficult horse to manage, gear might have broken or the saddle gone, but the fault always rested with you, the rider. The horse did not choose to be there. You are the chooser; the buck, so to speak, stops with you.

~

Gwen wrote to Mum on 3 May 1960 to thank her for the gifts Mum had included with the box of blankets sent for my swag: 'To-day we had our first letter from Roland—no doubt you have already heard from him. We are so relieved to hear that everything is up to expectations, & that the place is bristling with pythons and crocodiles. I told Roland before he left that I didn't want to know about the cows & kangaroos, I wanted to know about the people and the buildings. Of course his first letter is full of wildlife, but he says "I'll tell you about the blokes next time."'

I never did write to anyone about the blokes. We were in a relationship *to* each other rather than *with* each other. That may reflect many a workplace—particularly in the corporate world, with its adage that 'If you want a friend then get a dog'—but we lived together, ate together, slept near each other, worked from dawn to dusk on hard and often dangerous tasks then spent our Sundays off together. Still, we rarely got outside our skins and never talked about anything with depth or feelings around the campfire at night.

There were no work meetings or workshops of any kind about how to work better together or how to complete certain tasks in a coordinated manner. There were no strategic mustering plans that might be less hard on horses and men, no goal setting or vision statements.

Ralph Tate was aged about twenty and had left school in Cairns. He'd already had four years' experience as a ringer on a large cattle station managed by Reg's brother Des Nissen before he came to Augustus. Ralph was small and strong and often went shirtless in a blue workman's singlet to show it. He could come across as cocky, but he knew full well that I admired his skills. He played on that, but it only made me try harder.

Alan Candlish was a Cairns schoolfriend of Ralph's but a contrast in height and demeanour. He was tall and slim and had a reflective, deliberate step that mirrored his inner quiet. He'd had two years of experience at Rosella Plains Station, 320 kilometres north of Charters Towers, before joining Ralph at Augustus. His father had been killed in a mid-air collision over Borneo during the Second World War and Alan was a Legacy boy who had a softness about him. His mother sent him by the mail plane once a month a case of fruit, which he always shared with Ralph and me.

I was midway in height between Alan and Ralph. My big feet were noticed, and it was remarked that I would have been at least 190 centimetres tall if my growth had not been diverted horizontally. But height was never an issue among ringers because we spent most of our time on horses. The only time we worked on foot was in the bronco yards, where strength and a capacity to move quickly were important. I will tell you about bronco yards later.

We were all nicely elevated beyond what nature had endowed by Cuban-heeled R.M. Williams boots; there was little chance of getting caught up in the stirrups with Cuban heels. Every ringer wore them all the time, on foot or on horse, long before they became a fashion item, and sometimes to bed when we were on night-watch shifts for a few days and quietening a mob of about 1200 bullocks before handing them over to the drover for the 250-kilometre walk to the rail head at Kajabbi.

Of significant status was the camp cook, who had authority and knew it. The priority on arriving at every camp was to get the cook set up. The first cook I experienced, Peggy O'Neil, was a wizened little man with an unknown past who held the noble status of being a 'good bread cook', the standard by which camp cooks were judged.

Peggy spoke more to himself than to us; it's hard to know if he thought he was our friendly alarm clock or he was just plain mad. I woke to Peg's daily dawn chorus: 'Come on, Peg. On your wheels, old boy. These bastards have got to be fed, Peg. It's up to you and I, mate. They won't do it by themselves, Peg. There's no one else but you and I, Peg. It's always left to you and I, Peg. So let's get those wheels turning, Peg, old boy.' What on earth he said to himself all day alone in the camp I do not know.

We were attuned to the dawn, even without his mutterings, which always began before the birdsong; no alarm clock ever needed to ring. Daylight and dark set the time with or without Peg talking to himself. Most of us did not even carry a fob watch, the term used for a pocket watch carried on the belt.

Peg was later loaded onto a plane with a bad case of delirium tremens, the dreaded DTs. His secret rum cache had run dry, and the withdrawal it imposed on him sent him into a shivering gibberish. It turned out that those lively early morning conversations he'd held with himself were fuelled by a nip or two from a bottle of OP rum hidden in his swag. He was replaced by the diminutive Ted, who kept his false teeth in a cup of water all day to save wear and tear and only mounted them for the evening meal. Most of the time he went toothless all day, with his lips sucked in by the vacuum.

~

After only three months as head stockman, Jack McGynn was fired and left quietly without a goodbye. No best wishes for the future cards, no farewell party; I can't even remember saying goodbye. We were cold and compliant, or are they the same thing? Chances are we were out working when he left, and he drifted into the miasma of our short memories for people who came and went. Jack's legacy was my smoking; I could roll a cigarette and light it on horseback during the tired ride back after a long hard day.

Reg's son Fred took over as head stockman. Like his father, Fred was of average height. In his mid-thirties, he was in the prime of his life and had good looks and dark olive skin; handsome indeed under his Akubra Stetson. Fred, who was married and the father of a three-year old-boy, the only child on Augustus, was still recovering from a major horse accident that had kept him in hospital in Brisbane for many months about two years before my arrival. A horse had reared on him and his saddle, with the full weight of his horse on top of it, had broken his right arm and smashed his shoulder.

I am not sure if this was nepotism but he escaped the traditional obligation to take on the toughest of the horses to set an example for the rest of us. Fred now stuck to quiet horses, his favourite being a very tall skewbald gelding that was sedate and reliable. I look at photographs of our working horses at a camp, and if that skewbald horse is among them I know that Fred was head stockman at the time.

I had confusing terms to learn but everything had to be done quickly, with no time for a clarifying, 'Would you mind explaining that, please?' 'Bush the down-horned cow' referred to a cow with one horn cocked to the heavens, as was meant to be, and the other pointed towards the ground as if it possessed a permanent water diviner on that side; she had to be let back out to graze from where they had been mustered.

'Block that bloody stag' did not refer to any of the male deer in my childhood wildlife books. A stag was a male deprived of his testicles later in life, thus becoming a steer but retaining many of the outward characteristics of a bull. Testosterone had created its muscle distribution, but a stag could no longer deliver and was now destined to occupy a tin of corned beef with a key at its side—'key meat', as it is called in pidgin. Their dense muscle fibre holds the salt and sugar impregnated in them to help make them edible. That's where old bulls and stags go, instead of a comfortable superannuation on long grass.

Terminology became more complicated when it came to a 'mickey', which could refer to either a young bull just castrated or a young bull just beyond the calf stage. Walt Disney may have been a contributor to this usage, as 'Mickey Mouse' was often used as a derogatory term for an item of dubious origin.

Responding to these foreign commands was a major challenge during my first few months as they had to be understood and then coordinated with the precise response needed so as to ensure the animal with the minimum description attached to it reached its exact prescribed destination. Failure did not result in quiet acceptance of my inexperience, just a louder command. Being yelled at was also a great incentive to rapidly improve.

It could be very challenging when I got instructions to do different things in different places coming simultaneously from four different people. If I had trouble getting Strawberry to move fast enough or I wasn't sure what to do, I would be at the receiving end of: 'For Christ's sake, how many times have I told you: get around there and block them.' Or, for variety: 'For fuck's sake, just get out of the way and let me do it.'

I did not regard any of this as bullying—it was all about the task at hand—nor was there any indication that my employment was at risk. Perversely, the shouting indicated that I had potential and was really part of a team, just at the bottom rung of it. The result was that I demonstrated commitment like no other. No way was I going to stay at the bottom.

There was only one person who got under my skin. Les Rabbit constantly directed me to undertake actions I did not understand and could not have achieved even if understood; that was his tease. I was easily intimidated in those early days and could not tell him to shut up. Someone else should have told him to back off, but he was too cunning for that and saved his worst for me out of earshot behind a bellowing herd. My failure to meet his demands were followed by a 'Useless' and a shrug of his shoulders to indicate I was a total write-off. Rabbit was in his forties, making him an old ringer, so bitterness might have been his driving force.

Whenever we got back to the station to bring in steers from our muster and exchange horses, Rabbit would sit on the steps of the ringers' quarters after dinner and declare that 'The day of the west is fucked'. This was a frequent conversation he held with himself while patting Topsy, the blue heeler camp dog, when, with intent or coincidence, the sun was going down in the west. Perhaps Rabbit was proclaiming his expertise in predicting the strategic directions of the Gulf cattle industry; however, it was always within my earshot so undoubtedly I was highly complicit in the demise of the west.

Rabbit was alone in his disaster forecasting and none of the other ringers inquired about his accuracy. Maybe he was foretelling his imminent plane trip out, but for me, the day of the west was dawning and was full of promise.

8

DISTANCES

There was no gentle curvature of the earth in that low, flat Gulf Country. Even our widest and tallest horseback view in the open country was edged by lines of coolabah, tapping the underground water in shallow drainage lines. No rocky hill in the Top End provided any glimpse of a more distant horizon. Cattle did not climb them, so neither did we. The only way we could penetrate beyond our bounded horizon was by catching radio waves beneath the stars.

A typical Saturday evening: the meal done with and tomorrow our day off. Ken took his radio from its faded cream case, which was cracked into broken rivers of underlying brown. He uncoiled a thin, plastic-coated aerial wire, then, tying a rock to one end, he threw it over a nearby branch as a radio-wave trap. If no tree was handy the forked centre post holding up the cook's fly might do the job. A fiddle with the tuner and bingo! The ABC's Longreach Saturday night country and western request program entered our distant camp.

Illuminated by a carbide light, we sat on the ground or a drum or we leaned back against a partly rolled swag dragged over for the occasion. We were in contact with station people just like us—from western Queensland right across the Gulf Country and over to the Barkly Tableland in the Northern Territory. This was our world, and for this brief Saturday night we were connected to it.

We all treasured company, valuing it under the umbrella of music that reflected our lives. Our music overlaid ancient songlines we did not know existed. Old Davy, in the separate Aboriginal camp about 50 metres away, would have known those songlines, but he never acknowledged their existence to the deaf. Perhaps the Aboriginal ringers were listening in as the ABC drifted their way. Our songs were also about land and water. Drovers crossing flooded rivers on loyal horses. Faithful dogs saving lost children. Unrequited love.

No one sang along or talked beyond recognising names and places. Someone from Dalgonally Station had requested a Slim Dusty song and that got Ken talking about his days there. Names and stations rang bells of time, distance and past friendships. Each of us would disappear into that fog of the past soon enough, but right here and now, in the moment, we were one.

I learned a line or two so I could sing at the cattle, which had no choice but to listen. That was during the long hours on night watch, when cattle were quietened down for the drover. We sang or recited poetry or simply talked.

Saturday nights would be forgotten by Sunday morning, when we would share an open fire on which we boiled our clothes in kerosene drums. Sweat, bronco yard dust and blood on our clothes would create a thick, putrid, bubbling soup to which we might add a saddlecloth.

Ken shaved the black growth on his broad, open face. Under a wavy black mane he was fairly tall, but his powerful arms, attached to a deep barrel chest, made him appear closer to the ground. There was no slack in Ken, an all-round good-looking bloke. His favourite line was that he went to school once, then there was a well-judged pause before he added 'but the teacher was away that day'. His father had been a wool carter based in Julia Creek and Ken lasted just two years in primary school at Charters Towers before he absconded to drive a truck for his father. He was one of those people who had missed out on school but whose intelligence shone raw and direct.

Ken had replaced Fred as head stockman. He liked to talk about Julia Creek, with a special fondness for the big stations to its north; Millungera and Saxby Downs were his clear favourites. He spoke about the Flinders River, and the freshwater swordfish and small sharks that lurked in the oxbow lagoons that had been cut off as the river wound its way to the Gulf. He told how freshwater crocodiles travelled along the bore drains to find new territory. I liked his stories, but I didn't tell him that.

Ken was always asking someone to play cards on Sundays but I preferred mumblepeg, a traditional game in which two people sit cross-legged opposite each other with a smoothed patch of bare soil between them. A single pocketknife had to be stuck into the ground by a prescribed set of moves.

Sometimes a couple of us would sit and fish if we were camped on a waterhole.

Monday morning would come soon enough, and it might be my turn to get the horses in. That meant getting up at the crack of dawn without an alarm clock to tell me so, then I would walk to the horse yard at whichever camp we were based and catch and saddle the old night horse. He spent each night in the yard and did his grazing during the day. I would ride him out and run the horses in so they could be drafted for the day's work.

Burdekin duck, which is not remotely like any living thing let alone a wild duck, was a frequent breakfast. It is the quaint bushman's tradition of fried dough littered with small chunks of corned beef. Sometimes we got variety with a breakfast of sweet curry with dried sultanas. These were the main staples, only broken by fresh steak just after we'd killed. With no refrigeration and no capacity to age the steak in the kingdom of flies, this was so tough that mastication obliterated taste.

Every camp had a horse paddock with a rudimentary horse yard. After breakfast we would each select a morning horse and a dinner horse. Our morning horse might be a bit difficult to catch in the open or might put on a bit of a show and require mounting in the yard. Our dinner horse had to be caught and mounted in the open; it was necessary to provide a fresh mount for the afternoon.

The horses were run through the yards, with the morning horse caught by its rider as it was blocked. They would come through with a rush, a slip rail being used to divert the horse that had been nominated for the day into the saddling yard.

It was essential to block the horse by voice and presence and by standing in front of the slip rail before inserting it in its keepers.

Put simply: never be separated from the horse by the rail. Those horses that were not to be ridden that day would go 'bush', which meant they would be let through. A horse nominated for the day would be blocked with a slip rail while it was caught by its rider. Block the horse first and then insert the rail into its keepers while the person who has nominated it puts the bridle on if it is their morning horse. That was drummed into me, no doubt influenced by Leon's death. He had stood behind the slip rail to block a horse rushing to go into the bush yard. The horse hit the slip rail with such force that it broke into two with one piece flung back to hit Leon on the temple, killing him instantly.

The dinner horses would be drafted into a small holding yard ready for Joe Clifford, the horsetailer, who would take them to the place nominated for lunch and the horse exchange that day. After lunch Joe would bring the morning horses back and turn them out in the horse paddock; he would then bring the night horse in.

Joe had a certificate proving he was sane. Since none of us could furnish a similar qualification, he said our sanity remained in doubt. Joe had been conscripted for the Second World War but failed his medical on account of being mentally unfit. That tells you he was much older than us, but I knew nothing of Joe's life except that he had worked on a sheep station called Minnie Downs before arriving at Augustus long before me. Reg had found Joe a permanent niche as the camp horsetailer. Without Joe we would all have had to take turns at being the horsetailer and that would have taken a competent ringer out of action every day. Joe was handy and liked his role.

Unlike the rest of us, Joe only required two horses to do his job because they never had to exert themselves. That was also a saving, with fewer horses to take out to the camp. Joe's clear favourite was a bay mare he called Mischief, which he regarded as his best true friend. Tall, thin and uncoordinated, Joe leaned forward in the saddle in stirrups that were set way too long by our standards. He did not need speed, so his ungainly posture didn't matter. Even the gentle breeze from a trot folded back the brim of his ageing Akubra, as though it was an anchor to keep him in the saddle.

Once the horses were organised the head stockman would set out the day's mustering plan, although 'plan' is putting a sophisticated touch to a few words as to where we were headed for the day and who would go in which direction to get there. This meant that by lunchtime we would already have a sizeable herd gathered and we would take turns to keep them together while the others ate damper and corned beef and a cup of tea, all of which would have been carried to the designated site on a packhorse.

Managing a large mob of cattle demonstrates the absolute need for teamwork. Teamwork was never talked about; we just did it because there was no other way. It was understood without any need to talk about it. Kidman Brody owned the team; Reg, the station manager, was principal selector; the head stockman, who was now Ken, was captain-coach.

Well, maybe I should drop the 'coach' part as it was more accurately 'Captain Expectation'. It was the game that counted, anyway. Star players shone, and those playmakers made it easier for others. Every element in the structure was safe in its silo, no communication skills required. Action mattered.

Every camp had a small holding paddock large enough to hold a day's large muster of around 500 head or a couple of day's smaller musters, where they were held before branding in the bronco yard. Each camp had its bronco yard and within it a bronco ramp. Some stations at that time still had open bronco ramps where the cattle were held by men on horses while others did the branding.

Augustus had a wire bronco yard at each camp. The bronco ramp was set up at one end of the yard and consisted of two posts with a gap of about 10 centimetres between them. Attached to both posts was a panel of rails to another post about 2 metres away. The panel on the left-hand side as you faced it sloped down to about the height of a saddle's stirrup, so that when the bronco horse was ridden behind it the rope was on top of the sloping rail. The person on the bronco horse would ride out into the cattle to lasso a calf and drag it up to the ramp towards the sloping side. A turn to the left by the ringer on the bronco horse meant that the rope slid up the sloping rail and fell into the slot. The bronco horse was then ridden straight ahead and the calf pulled up to the ramp.

Meanwhile, us ringers on the ground would run out with green hide ropes and get the rope around the leg that would be furthest from the ramp. One team of perhaps one or two would get the lasso rope on the front leg and the other team on the back leg. The ropes would be on before the calf even reached the ramp and pulled tight and hitched around two wooden pegs at either end.

The two getting the front leg rope on were always competing with the two getting the hind leg rope on. You just wanted to be better, faster and smarter on your feet than anyone else. There was a sense of fun and achievement in getting through a big mob in a few hours. There was the musty-sweet smell of blood mixed with the smell of burning hair and hide from the hot branding iron. Old Davy inoculated each calf against pulpy kidney and black leg. As each calf was branded, it was also given the unique Augustus Downs earmark. The ringers on the bronco horse kept pulling up the cleanskins until there were none left.

The fine dust of the bronco yard was infused by the smell of blood and sweat from human and horse. All concentrated by the atmosphere of thousands of calves being cut, branded and earmarked on exactly that spot. Added together this created an overwhelming feeling of something good happening. It was more than the culmination of days on horses being bought to a natural conclusion. But you couldn't put a word to it and nor did we try. A cup of black tea if we finished the day did the trick.

We would be out on a stock camp for about four weeks before enough young steers had been accumulated by campdrafting them out from the mobs and all the branding was done for that area. It would then be time to head back to the station with the steers and to give our horses a spell and draft off new horses for the next camp. The fly neatly packed, the cook and all his gear, our swags and saddles for those of us not going back with the steers and horses and it was back to the station.

Our next job was to muster the Bullock Paddock. Its 155 square kilometres adjoined the Augustus boundary, where the stock route continued through Nardoo Station and stations beyond on the 192-kilometre walk to the railhead at Kajabbi for the train ride to steak at Townsville. It usually took three or four days to quieten the bullocks down before they were handed over to the drover, who usually only had one or two men on horses to assist and was in no position to manage a 'rush', the Australian version of a stampede . . . one of which I experienced.

~

Two mobs of 1200 each had already left Augustus and this was the last mob to go. We camped at the windmill yards and mustered enough bullocks for serious campdrafting that evening. Those selected were held in a large yard with big posts strung with wire that gave them space to lie down and get used to life on the road.

Night watch involved two ringers doing two-hour shifts, riding around the yard while singing, reciting poetry or in animated conversation with themselves or imaginary strangers. This was to let the cattle know we were there and to reduce the chance of one group getting a fright, which might happen if we rode around in silence and they suddenly awoke from a restless doze. These were not quiet cattle and this was their first experience of overnight captivity in confined quarters, but there was not a sound of complaint from them about our singing—or from any of the sleeping ringers, for that matter.

I always enjoyed my shifts of riding around the dark shape of the mob, with most of them lying down and chewing their cud on the open camp before handover. There were always two of us and that put heart and soul into the homily 'Sing as if no one is listening'. Augustus did not have night horses like the dedicated drovers did, but we could trust our horses enough to know they would prick their ears and look towards any bullock wandering off in the night.

I was sound asleep in my swag and due to be woken for my second watch when the bullocks rushed. They may have been startled by something as innocuous as one of the many Agile wallabies colliding with the fence, itself confused by the sudden appearance of so many cattle in its home range. The fright of the bullocks next to the disturbance instantly cascaded through the entire mob. The speed and panic of those bullocks in the dark made it impossible for Ken and Ralph, who were on watch, to follow them.

Dawn light revealed the mayhem: an entire side of the yard had been destroyed, with big coolabah posts cleanly broken off at ground level. There were five bullocks dead and another seven with broken legs or injuries that had to be shot. Those staged stampedes in the cowboy films I'd watched at the Civic, where twenty galloping cattle in broad daylight were outnumbered by cowboys on horses, were at least based on reality.

It took two days to muster the bullocks again and to draft out the replacement extras. We drove them to the Fourteen Mile Camp, a beautiful spot under bauhinia trees along the Leichhardt River. We tailed the bullocks out to graze during the day as if they were on the road. Watering them in the late evening involved getting them up and down the steep banks along the river, which was always dramatic and nerve-racking with 1200 head. They had previously dawdled quietly down to the water in fives and tens in single file, to drink slowly and then rest in the shade and swap yarns. When they were in one big mob they could become as stirred up as the water they were drinking.

The cattle were counted for the handover. We ran the mob through a gap between Reg and Logan Booth, the drover based in Burketown, each mounted on their horses counting the cattle running between them. We ringers created and then maintained a changing funnel so no bullock could dart around behind them. When they ran too fast or too many at a time, Logan and Reg would close the gap on their horses to slow them down then back off to allow a flow that suited their counting. They moved in and out without a word between them, as to speak would mean losing their count.

Our job was to feed the cattle through at exactly the right pace. Some of us continued to feed the dwindling group through while others rode to the other side of Reg and Logan to hold the growing mob that had been counted. Coordinating the count and managing the cattle required anticipating and executing the exact moment to move your horse into another position without a single word spoken between us.

It was beautiful to watch. There was a precision to it I did not think possible the first time I participated in the count.

I had assumed that with such a large mob of cattle the handover was just a close estimate, but it had to be accurate to the last beast because that was the basis of Logan's fee and the exact number of rail trucks had been ordered to be waiting at Kajabbi. Reg and Logan each had their favoured method of recording tens and hundreds on fingers extended and fingers bent. If the count between them did not agree it would be done all over again until they agreed on the exact number, but mostly they got it right in one count.

~

I have always regarded myself as a lucky person. Still do. Reg asked me if I would like to go with the cattle on to Kajabbi; in retrospect, he probably told me to do it. Anyhow, I jumped at the chance and can now say I went droving.

Logan had found himself shorthanded when one of his team became unavailable. There was only him and Jason, a young ringer who was probably a distant relative of his. Logan had to drive his truck loaded with our food, swags, spare saddlery and water.

The cattle were handed over at the Augustus boundary and it was all then up to Jason and me, with occasional help from Logan when he stopped the truck to provide us with lunch. The ten unridden drovers' horses became part of the mob and we slowly moved horses and cattle together, eating our way to Kajabbi. We travelled at 15 to 20 kilometres per day, depending on watering points along the stock route.

They were usually a bore with a trough that was fed from a turkey-nest holding dam by a windmill, although some waters were a regular dam, creek or lagoon.

Logan would meet us at lunchtime. Jason and I would snatch some sleep using the counter lining between the saddle flaps of our upturned saddles as a pillow while Logan tailed the cattle. My saddle was a well-shaped friend that fitted me as I fitted it. I perfected a lifelong ability to go to sleep immediately anywhere on anything.

The cattle became responsive and easy to manage by just the two of us: a quiet ride up one wing with a 'Move over, boys' here and there and the leaders would curve. When they changed direction they were followed by the entire mob. Logan pointed out a few landmarks each morning to help set the direction for the day. They could not be specific in such flat country, but they helped. After a week on the road the long stretch of low eucalypt and gidgee that went all the way to Kajabbi closed out the black-soil downs, so Logan parked the truck at shorter intervals to help us stick to the stock route through it.

Logan was totally relaxed about the whole venture and was a wonderful boss and mentor. He was a Burketown blend of Chinese, Aboriginal and Caucasian. There was never a sharp or anxious word from him or anything about him that created tension. I think his calmness rested deep within his complex racial mix. He felt totally at home among both Aboriginal people and the white station managers, being part of a distinct Gulf breed of men who had feet in many camps.

The three dedicated night horses, which were selected for night horse duty because they were very fast walkers that could get around a mob of cattle quietly and quickly, were never ridden during the day. They had to be easy to saddle and quiet to ride, because no flighty horse could concentrate on the task and it would not be a good idea for the rider to get distracted by having to manage a difficult horse in the night. After that, these horses needed to show some intelligence in spotting a wandering bullock in the middle of a dark night and to be able to take the initiative for the rider, who lacked their senses of smell and hearing.

One regular night wanderer never really gave up its quest to get back home. One black night he wandered off with three others from the opposite side of the mob to where I was at that moment. When I got around to that side my night horse simply did not want to continue going around the mob and insisted on walking out into the dark at a right angle. I was alone and perplexed. Each of us did a three-hour shift, and Logan and Jason were now asleep in their swags. I felt that the horse's instincts were superior to mine, so I let it have its head. It found those bullocks on its own, with me simply sitting on its back, and they were at least 300 metres away by the time we got around them and bought them back.

Every one of the bullocks was delivered to Kajabbi in ten days and loaded on the rail trucks for Townsville, where their journey ended. There was a certain satisfaction in completing a job well done but also a sense of loss, leaving a mob of cattle I had come to know so well. I returned to Augustus on the truck that carried bulk mail and stores from the railhead to the stations and to Gregory, on the way to Burketown.

Logan may have stayed on at Kajabbi to organise getting his horses back to Burketown.

The policeman from Gregory, who was returning from a Brisbane training session, shared the back of the truck with me. We sat high but comfortably on the load. From this vantage point he was able to hone the pistol shooting skills he had just upgraded in Brisbane. Between that and dozing, he counselled me on how easy it was to go downhill in the bush and that avoiding alcohol would help me prevent that decline. The next time I saw him was only a month later, at the Gregory races. Since I have little memory of the event, he may well have decided that his advice had not slowed my decline.

By this time the Gregory police station had a small lock-up but, before it was built, any intoxicated troublemaker got chained to a big old bauhinia tree outside the police station. Others would sneak alcohol to the chainee while the policeman was away patrolling the unruly mob; keeping the chainee inebriated ensured that the chain was unavailable for any other miscreant.

9

THE EMPIRE

Disraeli Camp was on the wild side: wild beauty, wild cattle, fast riding, danger. At 72 kilometres from the station, it was also the most distant camp on Augustus and so different from the open downs country where we spent most of the mustering season. Sandy Creek curved around red, rocky hills daubed with yellow spinifex. Springs seeping out of those hills kept the creek alive even in the driest of times, and Disraeli Camp was located on the bank of one of its big, crystal-clear lagoons.

When riding out to find scarce cattle we would pass along the broad, deep lagoons of Sandy Creek. I would listen for the soft swish and then I'd search for the ripple left by a crocodile disrupted from warming itself in the early sun. From horseback I could trace its underwater progress from the swaying waterlilies before it emerged in deeper water to watch through eyes it thought unseen. Disraeli had an innocent purity kept that way by those rocky hills and scrubby gullies doing their bit to control cattle numbers.

One evening as we returned to camp at Disraeli, Ted, the cook who had replaced Peggy, shouted to us from across Sandy Creek that he had just killed 'a taipan'. I dismounted faster than anyone else, dropped the reins of my unsaddled horse and ran around the head of the waterhole to cross its shallows and reach the excited Ted. He proudly displayed a magnificent three metre specimen of a dead Olive python. Gutted, I pointed out his error.

Ted was without remorse, and proud of his accomplishment. Seething with anger, I wondered how it was possible to be that fucking stupid. I could not stand the sight of him with the dead python and had to walk away to avoid irreparable conflict with the person who fed me. Others arrived to see Ted's dead 'taipan', and just shrugged their shoulders with a 'so what?' when I told them it was a harmless Olive python.

Disraeli was the only camp with such a distinct name. The next camp in towards the station was Smith's Yards, probably built by a bloke called Smith, followed by the Twelve Mile Camp. Fiery Camp was a former outstation that was named after Fiery Creek, most of which ran through flat country that reduced it to disconnected muddy waterholes in the dry. Further in, and only 30 kilometres from the station, was Dinner Camp Bore, which was equipped with the only windmill on Augustus. Boundary Camp was 20 kilometres away by road but only two hours by horseback. That had consequences that I will tell you about later. Then there were the two closest camps, the Steer Paddock and the Bullock Paddock.

Someone had stamped 'Empire' on Disraeli, but who did that stamping? Was it John Costello, who became the first white person to claim squatters' rights on Mingin country and called it Augustus Downs after the explorer Augustus Charles Gregory, or was it Oscar de Satgé, the English would-be aristocrat who led the syndicate that later purchased it from Costello? More about those two characters in Chapter 11.

Every camp had a structure over which the canvas fly could be erected immediately upon arrival. The carefully folded canvas fly was thrown over a permanent pole supported by two forked posts and rolled out, then stretched out and tied to poles that ran its length on both sides that were mounted on shorter forks. Each camp also had a rudimentary horse yard, a horse paddock and a bronco yard for branding within a holding paddock. Once the fly was up, a folding wooden table was erected near one end and the cook lit his fire at the other end. There would always be enough wood left behind from the last time the camp had been used to get the fire going straight away. Large tins of flour, cases of tinned tomatoes and jam plus a bag of potatoes and pumpkin were stored under cover along each side.

We craved that first cup of tea, black, 'just like our girls'. But that was bullshit: there was this thing about not getting too close to Aboriginal people. The water at Dinner Camp Bore tasted foul. At this camp alone, out of the many on Augustus, Kidman Brody Pastoral Company allowed us to have instant coffee on account of the water defying any attempt to make drinkable tea.

With a fire going to produce coals under the camp oven, water would be boiled up in a four-gallon flour drum to produce a quick meal of potato and pumpkin, accompanied by salted brisket bubbling fat to the surface. Lacking comfortable fold-out camp chairs, we might sit on the ground or on the flour drums or steel water containers called 'canteens' that were moulded to fit the shape of a horse when mounted on a pack saddle. They were rarely mounted on saddles but did serve as the main source of water for the cook.

The tent fly was illuminated by a single carbide light. There was a small metal container about the size of a large jam jar filled with lumps of calcium carbide. A larger metal sleeve had a long stem at one end fitted over it with enough of a rim to hold water that dripped slowly into the calcium carbide to produce acetylene gas, which rose in the long stem. The gas was then lit to produce a bright light. There was lots of talk about the risk of the hole at the end of the stem getting clogged and producing an explosion that would send it through the fly roof, but I never witnessed that occur. Still, it was recommended that we should never stand over this contraption.

We often killed a beast for meat when we arrived at a camp. There was no refrigeration of any kind for keeping fresh meat, even at the station meat house. We killed about once a month, in the afternoon following a shorter day of mustering. The killed animal never carried the Augustus Downs brand, easily identified by an earmark; the primary qualification was that it was a 'stranger', carrying the earmark and brand of a neighbouring station. As they said: 'If you want to taste your own beef then go to your neighbour's place for dinner.' Eating your neighbour's cattle probably balanced out and no one was worse off.

'Poddy dodging'—the euphemism for cattle duffing—was a different matter. Sometimes it involved a liberal application of your brand on the calf of a cow that bore next-door's brand and earmark. It got more serious at the Top End. On one occasion Ken, Alan and I came across a recently built and heavily used set of hidden yards in a remote area near the Augustus boundary. The risk of being caught was reduced if they knew there was no one at our Twelve Mile Camp. Branded and earmarked cattle were not their target; there were plenty of cleanskins to label. They would then blend them with a quiet mob of coachers and drive them to another destination, which may have been through and beyond the next-door property.

The evening meal might be followed with a bit of lying on the ground around a separate outside fire, but often we were dead on our feet and ready for our swags.

A water bag hung in the shade of the fly to catch the breeze for some evaporative cooling. Sometimes we came into camp so thirsty we gulped water poured into the quickly flattened crown of our hats. A parched thirst would have us drink from the muddiest of waterholes, from some of which protruded the skeletons of cattle that had died at the end of the previous summer dry before the monsoon rains arrived. Nothing could deter an aching thirst.

'Did you have a wash?' meant that you were suspected of coming to breakfast, lunch or dinner without scrubbing your hands in the tin wash basin. Ringers took pride in cleanliness, with good reason, and there were no shared colds or flu. The lumpy and unglamorous bar of Velvet soap was the basic personal hygiene essential. It also had the advantage of being easily shaved into slivers with a pocketknife so it could go into a four-gallon drum over a fire to wash our clothes.

There was no digging a toilet pit or latrine. If you needed a piss you walked beyond the swags but you went further for a crap, carrying a shovel and a toilet roll and burying the results. This worked because we were few and only stayed at each camp for five to eight days.

Dingoes regard human faeces as an irresistible delicacy, so they probably dug up our deposits and feasted on them. This was before the use of 1080 (sodium fluoroacetate) really took off and dingoes were common. Some ringers had a bottle of strychnine to lace a few bones after killing a beast for meat. Any dingo found dead would be scalped and taken to the station, where the bounty would be paid into their wage by Reg, who would then be reimbursed by the government.

With a distinct and long dry season, we slept under the stars without tent or cover. Rolling a cigarette-thin swag was admired as it was still common enough to carry them on a packhorse. Being our personal domain, our swags became our retreat, our cold night comfort and our home. My sheet of canvas was folded over and sewn to create a pocket for my clothes that doubled as a pillow. All that separated me from the ground was a thin underlay blanket. I kicked smooth any lumps and, if they persisted, I would break off some thin leafy branches or pluck some grass to even them out. At dawn I folded the flaps over the blankets or loosely rolled it up to offer some protection from dust.

Augustus was a dry station: there was no ration of beer at night or even on the weekend. The alcohol ban may not have withstood a legal challenge, not that it mattered: Reg was god, and any alcohol consumption would have you on the next plane out. We did not talk about such things, let alone discuss or reflect on the pros and cons. Maybe the other ringers were pleased to comply with the alcohol restriction, because it meant someone else made the decision for them to stay healthy and sober and it even allowed them to save some money. Often that saving went into a big bender at the end of the year, so alcohol got it one way or the other.

I enjoyed the camps at Top End and the mustering there the most. There were two- and three-year-old unbranded cleanskins, together with a variety of older cattle that might have only seen the yards when they were branded. If a male calf managed to accidentally miss castration and keep its testicles, then testosterone would promote rapid growth of its bone and muscle until maturity puts a brake on further growth. This would give it the powerful and strong body of a bull. Male calves that are castrated to become steers but then are missed in subsequent musters, avoiding the journey to steak, just keep growing. Without that testosterone brake they become giant eunuchs as tall as a horse. They get the unprepossessing title of 'piker bullocks' because of their disposition to lie down and die once they are thrown, dehorned and yarded.

Mustering at the Top End camp consisted of trying to get a small group together as coachers—cattle already mustered that could be controlled—for any of the wilder cattle. Old Davey would ride in front; he could track a single beast at a fast trot if it had seen us or smelt us and disappeared into the scrub. When that animal was found, an exhilarating and dangerous gallop would ensue through dense scrub. If ringing them as group failed, we would take off individually or in pairs after the most valuable recalcitrant.

Horsebacking was the safest method of throwing them and tying their hind legs with bull straps, but this required a quick decision by two riders and a highly coordinated response between them. The leading rider leaned from his horse to grab the beast by the tail while it was in full flight, then he let the tail run through his hand to its tip to gain maximum leverage. He would then get up extra speed and make a sudden 80- to 90-degree turn away from the direction he and the beast had been travelling. This would cause the beast to fall and roll over having lost its balance from the momentum and power transferred through the held tail.

The person on the second horse needed to follow close behind and jump off quickly and take hold of the upper hind leg of the downed beast before it could get up. Holding that leg up as high as possible, it would control the biggest and strongest bull or bullock. The other horseman would return and take a bull strap worn around his waist to tie together its two back legs. Horsebacking was difficult to achieve in the dense scrub and its limitation was that it needed two people, when everyone might have split in different directions and be busy chasing strays.

The alternative, and by far the most common method, was for a single ringer to keep up with the fleeing beast until it started to get exhausted. After being followed at speed for a few hundred metres it would turn around and threaten to charge the horse and rider. This is where spurs became important, and we only wore them in the Top End to get ourselves and our horses out of the way when the bovine victim resorted to charging. That, however, was part of the plan. As you backed your horse off the beast would turn to escape, and before it could gather any pace you would jump off your horse, run up and grab it by the tip of its tail.

It sounds difficult, but it is easier than you might imagine. The immediate response of the animal was to turn around and charge you. Just as it turned and had both of its back feet off the ground, you would take an almighty pull on its tail so it lost balance and toppled over. Both hind legs were tied together by a bull strap, a single bull strap in my case, but there were those who wore two and Les Cockerill would wear three and use them all on three different beasts. Throwing cattle was not regarded as foolhardy or unnecessary risk taking, and was just part of the skill set. In earlier times, some head stockmen on northern stations carried a pistol, with more drastic consequences for those intransigents that could not be restrained.

Having thrown a beast, you needed to remember where the strapped animal was and go and find everybody else before coming back to collect it with the coachers. Normally the thrown beast would have its horns cut off before being released among the coachers. Sometimes the big piker bullocks would just not get up at all and were left to die. At other times the recently thrown animal, with blood flowing from the stumps where its horns were, would be content to fall in with the coachers. It was always a terrible disappointment to throw a huge piker and get it back to the yard then have it lie down and die overnight, but this was not uncommon.

Between Disraeli and the station on the Leichhardt River lay Augustus Downs' huge breeder country, which had no fences dividing it into paddocks. Indeed, much of the Augustus Downs' boundary remained unfenced and cattle stayed in their familiar mobs on water and that served as a form of boundary management. They were 'hefted' to Augustus by its water and grass, using the term so eloquently applied by James Rebanks in describing how sheep congregated according to their individual home farm among the many other flocks also running on the commons. Such insight defied our days when taking so much for granted and we mustered without thought that during any one day we were probably accumulating a big mob made up of many different groups that allocated themselves a slice of the grass cake and bucket of water in places of comfort. It was precisely those groups, stuck to place, that needed shifting to other water when their waterholes ran dry.

The whole of Augustus Downs was 3107 square kilometres; its breeder country carried on average 15,000 head of shorthorn cows and was 2226 square kilometres, or 70 per cent of the entire area. The breeder country was like a giant funnel, through which the Steer Paddock, the Bullock Paddock and the Spayed Cow Paddock were topped up each mustering season. Each of those paddocks was 155 square kilometres, or 60 square miles as we knew them then. The actual area of the Spayed Cow Paddock was somewhat reduced by horse paddocks, the station surrounds and the airstrip paddock.

A spayed cow was one that had had its ovaries removed by Reg so she could concentrate on putting on condition and not entertaining bulls and experiencing the joys of motherhood. There was no detectable genetic strategy in deciding which heifers should be spayed from among the breeding herd; it was up to the head stockman to make the decision and bring them in with the steers to the station yards for Reg to perform his surgery. The only consistent characteristic that sent a cow to be spayed was a general dislike for any shorthorn cow that had a black muzzle compared to the preferred pink muzzle. It remains a mystery as to how the colour of a cow's muzzle could impact on its fecundity and milking ability. Who knows how many genetically superior and profitable heifers were dispatched by Reg's surgery.

Reg cut a slice in the cow's flank just behind the end of her ribcage and inserted his hand to locate the closest fallopian tube. He would follow this until he had an ovary between his fingertips, then he would insert an emasculator with his other hand. Its blades would snip the tube, and behind the blades was a flat section that crushed the tube to prevent bleeding. Out came the ovary and then, using the same opening, Reg would find the other ovary and repeat the process. The wound would be stitched up and covered with a daub of fly repellent tar and—bing!—that was it, all done in less than three minutes. Reg kept this skill to himself and never mentored a junior surgeon. I guess he thought it was a waste of time because we would all move on. We were a compliant group that was kept that way by never complaining or even asking to widen our skill base.

The head stockman determined whether a male calf became a steer singing with the castratos or remained intact to roar and paw and grind the ground with the bulls. There were no breeding or performance records to confuse the head stockman in making those choices. This meant there was a bias towards selecting older calves as bulls, because the young ones were difficult to assess. Not many bulls were required because the bull-to-cow ratio was supposed to be around four bulls to a hundred cows but, since there were no paddocks, it meant the bulls could wander around to please themselves and congregate for meetings in better country or around water, and neglect those hardy cows that walked out far and wide.

We were in the saddle every day. Usually it was at least a twelve-hour day stretched over two horses. Even on branding days two people were on horses in the bronco yard and the rest of us were on horses as they were let out. We held them for an hour or so to give the calves a chance to mother up.

~

We were without curiosity as to what transpired in the heads of the horses we rode. We could not tell what was going on in the minds of our colleagues and they were the same species as us, so how on earth would it be possible to know what transpired in the mind of your horse? It was the same way we judged each other: at face value. We considered our horse's heads about as much as we peered into each other's heads, but we all got along fine except for the odd argument or two. And that was no different with our horses.

At the same time, any sign of cruelty was sanctioned and a ringer being hard on his horse would see him cautioned. One of those hardnesses might be jerking the horse's mouth if it made a wrong turn or did not appear capable of making a sharp turn. Another frowned upon habit was using a stick to make your horse go if it was exhausted—'knocked up', as we described it. Using a slap of the reins was acceptable, but anything more than that elevated it to comment level. There were never clear criteria established as to what level of encouragement entered the 'hard on a horse' category, but you were expected to know it and feel it when a horse could give no more.

A bit of history followed every working horse from the time it was freshly broken in. Words of caution might be offered based on the past behaviour of a horse, but this was always just a warning rather than the description of an unmalleable trait. The horse might behave in a diverse way either because you did something differently or because it was one year older now and behaved differently. One of the ringers who had been on the station long enough to observe the horse just allocated to your team might say, 'Watch out when you're saddling Flight, that bastard will cow kick you while you're doing up the girth.'

It was not long after Ken became head stockman that we camped at the Fourteen Mile Camp in the Bullock Paddock to get the second lot of 1200 bullocks ready for the drover Logan Booth. It had taken us three days to gather up the required number of bullocks, and it was going to take us another three days to quieten them down sufficiently to hand over to Logan and his team of two.

The bullocks were being tailed out, feeding about a kilometre from the camp, and I went back in for lunch and to
change horses. After a lunch of cold corned beef and pickles
on warm damper and a pannikin of black tea, I walked over
to the yards; Strawberry had been held for me there along
with the other dinner horses. My riding had improved, but
I was frustrated that I was never able to move Strawberry
beyond a slow walk to a trot at best. I reckoned a pair of
spurs might induce a more sprightly attitude from him. We
all had a set of spurs reserved for the Top End and I got mine
out for Strawberry in the hope that I could get him out of a
walk and minimise any criticism for being slow off the mark.

I was correct about the spurs, but Strawberry had different
ideas. I mounted him with my spurs jangling and immediately sensed a seismic shift in this aged skeleton. With his ears
back, he put his head down between his legs and bucked high
into the air, coming down on all fours so hard that it jolted
me loose even in the soft, sandy yard. As Strawberry twisted
under me, I swapped my saddle for dust.

I had by now ridden horses that bucked or pig-rooted
straight ahead. They were crow hoppers—horses that give a
small buck by kicking their legs back—and there was no credit
given to riding them. But no crow hopper came anywhere near
Strawberry's skill set of going up high and then coming down
with a bone-jarring jolt, followed by a sharp twist before
bucking high again in another surprising direction.

The whole thing was watched by the ringers who had come
in for lunch. Interest in my next move overrode any concern
for my physical or psychological welfare, but to their great

credit they watched in silence without giving advice or egging me on. Not to be shamed, I got straight back on Strawberry with my spurs still on and he launched into it again, but his dose of youthful determination had waned somewhat after the first explosion and I managed to ride him this time.

Strawberry and I joined the mob of cattle, with me feeling nervous every time those spurs made the slightest tinkle. Strawberry put his ears back every now and then, but the poor old thing was probably exhausted from his previous efforts to get rid of the vexatious person wearing them. It was quiet work tailing the bullocks, keeping them in a loose mob as they grazed, but the problem was that Strawberry also rested. I felt him stirring under me and saw another battle looming, with me being thrown again by this old warrior. This time it would be away from the soft sandy yards, and I would have to walk back or get someone to chase after him. I decided it was a good idea to dismount and put the troublesome spurs in my saddlebag. The aged Strawberry had beaten me.

No one said anything to my face at dinner, except a few stray remarks about getting thrown and what good entertainment it provided. Somewhat tired, I turned in early. As I lay in my swag I could hear them talking about me around the campfire. Today's Strawberry episode provided endless variations for the telling, and the campfire conversation revealed that Strawberry had been a difficult horse to ride when he was young and had been renowned as an accomplished bucking bronc when something sparked him off. When he was allocated to me they had thought that, with age, he was well over it.

They liked the way I got back on him immediately and was able to ride him during his next bucking session: 'The young fella is coming on. Did you see the way he kept up with him?' I could hear Ralph say, 'He sat right up front of the saddle, like he was going to stay there.' Followed by a muffled, 'He's got some guts, the way he got straight back on.' And so it went on while I laid there under the pretence of sleep and loving every minute of it.

Strawberry and I resumed our previous relationship, with him walking and me urging him on with my voice and the odd slap of the reins along his thin, bony neck, but I had to be content with whatever speed that accomplished. Strawberry went into retirement soon after, and still lives ever so fondly in my memory of that wonderful time of my life.

10

THE ABORIGINAL RINGERS

'You go around behind that patch of gidgee and start them, and I will pick them up this side.' That was the sort of interaction between Black and white. I didn't know them although they worked with us day in and day out, mustering from the start of the season to the end of season. They lived a separate life to us. That is why they're in a separate chapter. It should have been different. Here I was enjoying the best of times on what had been, such a short time ago, their land.

There was a long period of tolerance once the squatters, assisted by troopers and government policies, had defeated Aboriginal resistance. After that, many stations had a large Aboriginal camp of men, women and children to draw upon for cheap labour. When the stations became hard pressed during the Great Depression, they sought to remove the Aboriginal families. Now driven by economic imperatives, they resented supplying the odd bullock to the Blacks' camps, enforcing peace among various factions that had been disrupted by the white invasion and providing emergency medical assistance for the sick and injured.

So began the era of the removalists, which included Augustus Downs. Most of those removed from Augustus were sent to Doomadgee near Burketown or Mornington Island, a period that lasted well into the late 1950s. One of many hundreds of records kept by the Queensland government lists the 1927 removal of Kitty and her children Gracie (aged eleven), Gladys (eight) and Mavis (two), and the children of Topsy (deceased) named Thelma (six) and Muriel (four) from Augustus Downs and sent to Mornington Island Mission in the Arafura Sea, 137 kilometres out from Burketown.

The Lardil are the traditional owners of Mornington Island, but the removalists were unconcerned about the social conflicts they were causing by mixing different language groups in the close confinement of the missions. Queensland was an active removalist along with the other states and the Northern Territory.

King Davy—or 'Old Davy' or 'Old Man' as he was variously called—was on Augustus long before Reg Nissen. There is a photo of him taken by Alfred Amos, valet to the governor general, the Duke of Gloucester, during his visit to Augustus Downs in June 1946. It shows a handsome, strong Davy who looks to be well into his forties. He had been presented with a king plate, known as a 'gorget', by the Queensland government. The aim of awarding king plates was to provide a role model for other successful assimilation.

We accepted that Davy was a king because he acted like royalty. He was an elder of any one of the Maga-Kutana,

Wakabunga, Nguburinjo, Ganggalida or Mingin language groups in the large catchment of the Gregory River. I like to think I was riding with a Mingin on his own country. Davy was always incredibly useful and remained on Augustus after the removalists had been through.

Davy was said to be around eighty years old when I arrived in 1960 and, if so, he was still incredibly fit and strong; he worked on horseback from dawn to dusk just as we did. He was still tall, with daylight showing between widely bowed legs that accentuated their separation and led my eye to each foot, connected squarely to the ground.

Davy plaited the neatest and strongest green-hide ropes of anyone on the station, until it got to the stage where no one else even bothered and they were all made by him. He could track wild cattle and at a fast trot if their tracks showed they had been startled by the sound or smell of us. Davy often rode in front when we were up in the station's Top End, with Ken a pace behind him and the rest of us following in adrenaline-fuelled anticipation. It was a grand sight. My heart would pump faster, my legs tautened to stand in the stirrups and my reins collected for a fast gallop through thick scrub.

~

By my time on Augustus Downs the missions had become recruitment agencies for Aboriginal ringers. If the station ran short of 'boys', Reg would send a telegram through the flying doctor channel to the missions at Mornington Island and Doomadgee requesting replacements. The mission adminis-trators decided who went where. It was not entirely despotic, because some Aboriginal men and women preferred work on stations to boredom and to earn a little extra for their families. Although it was no compensation for their loss, it was also a way Aboriginal people could get back to the country from which they had been removed.

There were others who would have liked to have gone, but they were reluctant to leave their wives and children behind. The demand for men outstripped the need for station domestics, so very few Aboriginal ringers got to live with their wives and children. Percy was the only Aboriginal ringer on Augustus accompanied by his wife, but I rarely saw her as she went to the big house early in the morning and glided back silently at dusk.

The Aboriginal 'boys' arrived at Augustus on the TAA DC-3 or the freight truck that ran between Burketown and Kajabbi. Far from being boys, they ranged in age from twenty to forty and they all had some prior experience on cattle stations. The missions fitted them out in brown cotton trousers with an army disposal look and new blue work shirts that were made even bluer by their dark faces. Their skins were unblemished by the same sun and wind that lashed the faces of the white ringers. Their hats had a proud personal bash, indicating they had been in use for longer than the rest of their fresh standard-issue mission clothing.

A rigid pattern of living kept our cultural separation in place. I worked alongside the Aboriginal ringers every day, but I knew none of them as people who shared my world. They lived in small one-roomed tin huts on concrete slabs that were conveniently located just behind the horse yards and over 200 metres from the white ringers' quarters.

We never ventured near their huts and knew nothing of how they lived: whether they had iron beds with mattresses or simply rolled out their swags on the floor; whether there was a hierarchy among them. Did they sit around an open fire and open cans of baked beans and spaghetti in tomato sauce purchased from the station store, or did they cook catfish and wallaby to supplement their rations? No such questions crossed our minds.

My childhood German outsider experience was shelved and provided no empathy for this other culture on my doorstep. I wanted to belong to my group. There was no induction or training to show us how new white ringers such as me should relate to Black ringers. This was not considered necessary because a legislative barrier stronger than any brick wall kept us from crossing into Black territory. The lives of Aboriginal ringers were governed by the 'act', and that established an impenetrable barrier between them and us.

We knew nothing about the act since legislation of any kind lay well outside the language of cattle and horse work, but Aboriginal disadvantage was set in concrete by the Queensland Aboriginals Protection and Restriction of the Sale of Opium Act 1897. It made Aboriginal people wards of the state of Queensland, without any right to British citizenship as it was at the time of the Act. The Act defined 'Aboriginal' in the broadest possible terms and included a wide variety of racial mixes, such as Caucasians, Chinese and Afghan cameleers. It controlled every aspect of their lives, from where to live to how much they should be paid and their indemnity relationships with employers.

There was a long history of Aboriginal stockmen on Augustus Downs and an earlier manager had expressed a preference for them, because 'if you can get them young they are much easier to knock into shape than white blokes'. The removal of Aboriginal people from the stations had meant the missions had more control; they no longer sent very young and inexperienced men to be shaped, and some station managers lamented the ease with which Aboriginal ringers could now return to the mission when they were even slightly dissatisfied.

The Aboriginal ringers at Augustus had a lot to be dissatisfied about, but this was never apparent to me since they worked with enthusiasm and commitment and were an integral part of the team. There was no intended or unintended racism that I recall; it was simply not necessary to compare or compete with them because racial disadvantage was firmly embedded by the Act and we were securely on the other side of it. I heard no outward disrespect towards the Aboriginal ringers from any of the head stockmen I worked under, nor did any of the ringers treat them any differently when we were working cattle.

There was, however, one racial stereotype that I presume was pervasive throughout the northern stations. It held that you should avoid sending two or more 'Blackfellas' out mustering together because 'as soon as they get out of sight, they will start looking for dingo pups to scalp to earn the bounty'. I did not witness any of them doing this, and if they did it was obviously a consequence of their economic circumstance. Old Davy did spend his weekends tracking dingoes to their pups in hollow logs and other hidden places to earn the meagre bounty handed out by Reg on behalf of the government. I recall him proudly showing me the tiny little scalps of six dingo puppies.

There was another incident that involved dingoes. Ken, Davy and I were mustering along a dry creek bed out at Smith's Yards Camp while the others were picking up cattle out wider. We heard whimpering from the creek bed and rode down to see three dingo pups, about a month old, whose mother had probably taken off in fright at our presence. Each of us picked up a pup. I was holding mine gently, patting it and wondering how I could get it back to camp.

Ken grabbed one pup by the hind legs and dispatched it with a sharp hit on the head on a nearby tree. Davy did the same, his with equal rapidity. Since I was not participating in this execution, Ken said, 'Give it here.' Sensing the inevitable I did so, and the scalp of my future pet joined those that Davy had already scalped and put in his saddlebag. We continued mustering as if it had never happened.

Aboriginal ringers were cheaper to run than us, and we were cheap enough. In 1960, my first year at Augustus, the full award rate for a white stockman over the age of twenty-one was the equivalent of $32 per week today. The award rate for an Aboriginal stockman between the ages of eighteen and forty-five was $16.50 per week; if he was over forty-five and regarded as active his weekly wage declined to $15 per week, and if he was classed as not active by the station manager it reduced to approximately $11 per week.

The role of the non-active Black ringer was supposed to be doing odd jobs around the station, but there was no such position on Augustus, where it was either cattle and horse work or back to the mission. The Aboriginal ringers were allowed approximately $3 per week of their wage to purchase essentials from the station store. That meant the station ended up with what they got paid anyway. Most of the remainder went back to the mission, with the exception of between 2.5 and 10 per cent, depending on the size of family and location, which went into the Aboriginal Welfare Fund established by the Queensland government in 1943.

The Aboriginal people would one day lay claim to that fund with varying degrees of success and without full compensation. The result of the wage differential on Augustus Downs was that Aboriginal ringers received half the total income of the white ringers and only received as a discretionary income about one seventh of the wage earned by their white counterparts. Then the station got some of their money back, of course, by having the only shop in town for soap, tobacco and some other essentials.

When we were at the station the white ringers sat down at a table next to the kitchen, where we served ourselves. By contrast, the Aboriginal ringers came to an opening on the side of the kitchen where there was a window with a hinged corrugated-iron flap propped open. Here the cook served out their meal on a tin plate and filled their large tin pannikins with black tea. They carried these back to their huts and there were no second helpings.

On the stock camp the Aboriginal ringers rolled out their swags some 50 to 100 metres away from us and had their own campfire. At the sound of the dinner bell they walked over to the fly and the cook served dinner out to them, whereupon they would disappear into the night. They rarely got a second helping.

What I have described here was typical of the Gulf stations, but there was, of course, great variety in the way whites and Blacks worked together. I learned from others that on remote cattle stations in the Kimberley and on Cape York Peninsula that the only white person in the cattle camp might be the head stockman. He and the Aboriginal ringers lived together while out on camp, but on their return to the station they would reassume their traditional separation and the head stockman would eat in the big house kitchen while the Black ringers returned to their camp by the river nearby.

~

Johnson Charles was tall and powerfully built with an easygoing nature. He became very close to Old Davy, and they spent a lot of time together; perhaps they were from the same language group. Johnson was very capable, but there was every chance that Davy was mentoring him in how to work well alongside the white blokes. Johnson got more responsible roles such as riding the bronco horse and lassoing. It was the relationship between Davy and Johnson that saved me on one occasion from serious injury or losing my life.

When the first mob of scrubbers we tracked one early morning at Disraeli Camp split in all directions, I took off on Sultana after a very fast and agile three-year-old cleanskin bull in the prime of his life. I followed my bull at a gallop through dense scrub for about 500 metres, until it tired and turned to charge me and my horse. I held Sultana off until the bull turned to escape and that was my moment to jump off and run to grab its tail.

This strong young bull would not lift either of his hind feet off the ground, keeping his considerable strength and weight on all four legs as he spun around and around, lunging with his pointed horns and doing his best to rid himself of the pest holding his tail. They were shorthorn cattle, but fucked if I know how they acquired that title—probably in comparison to Texas Longhorns—but these shorthorns had horns sufficient to wound or kill a human. This bull was bellowing and slobbering at the mouth from his tiring gallop while turning to try to hook me with its sharp horns. I was reasonably safe provided I held his tail at full length. Giving up and letting go carried some risk, as he might not immediately appreciate his victory.

Getting tired, I let some more tail slip through my hand to gain longer leverage. In desperation I only held his tail by its very tip. A mighty pull when I thought his two hind legs might have been off the ground reduced the distance between us enough for him to make a lunging hook and get one horn between my legs. He reefed his horn right up to my groin and tossed me high in the air.

I came down on my back, with the bull grinding my chest into the ground with his forehead ready to do serious damage with his horns. I was a clichéd rag doll. It might also be a cliché to say that I really thought my life was over, but that was the case: *Roland, you wanted to be a cowboy, and now it's over.*

Suddenly, Johnson and Davy popped up out of nowhere and rammed the bull with their horses, until it forgot about me and took off into the scrub. Free for another year at least, if not for life. Completely unhurt and fully recovered in moments, I got back on my horse. The three of us rode to find the others, who had managed to ring a small mob of older cows with calves that would be used as coachers to go and pick up those that Ralph and Ken had thrown.

I might have mentioned my little adventure around the campfire that night but, if so, it was nothing out of the ordinary, nothing that would not have been expected of me or that could not be topped by their experiences that day. I bear no scar, no bruise; I just have a memory to remind me, when I read in the press or hear on the news that someone has been injured or killed by a bull, that Davy and Johnson probably saved me from serious injury or worse.

~

George Wing was a 'yella fella', the now offensive term then used for Aboriginal people of mixed background. Most were under the Act but George had, as the saying went, 'got out from under the act' and therefore joined us in the ringers' quarters and lived with us. The minister could grant a certificate of exemption under the Act. Obtaining such a certificate involved overcoming many impediments. Few Aboriginal people were able to understand the provisions of the Act let alone write an application for exemption that might pass the scrutiny of the chief protector. The only other opportunity was to find someone else to write the application.

Each application had to be accompanied by character references, which were not easy to obtain from white people who mattered. However, many Aboriginal people who were categorised as 'half-caste' in the Act had learned to read and write when taken from their families as part of the stolen generations, and they had white contacts such as teachers and wardens to act as referees.

As a 'yella fella' in our ringers' quarters, George Wing was a person between two worlds. There is every chance he was a victim of the Stolen Generations. He did not belong to the Aboriginal ringers and neither did he belong among us. Out from under the Act, he was left high and dry as an in-between man. George was tall and powerful, good looking and scrupulously well dressed in his ringer clothes. He was totally competent and quietly confident, and totally ignored.

George was also a victim of Les Rabbit's deviousness, but I was never sure of the circumstances. George had writing skills that had no doubt assisted his application to the chief protector, and he wrote a poem about Rabbit in a neat flowing longhand. He gave me the original before he left us quietly without a word of farewell.

Perhaps George reckoned that, because I was also a victim of Rabbit's venom, I was someone who might one day understand his situation. However, I like to think that I might have shown George some friendship tinged with an inkling of empathy and that is why he gave me the only copy of his handwritten poem, which I still have. George referred to Rabbit as the 'shadow', and his poem began:

Be careful when you're talking
That the shadow's not around
For his ears are protruding
When he hears the slightest sound.

If you're running down the station
And you know that things aren't quite right
Make sure and have a look around
That the shadow's not in sight.

George's poem ended with these words:

Tis said he has a hobby
Of getting men the sack
And if he takes a set against you
You can bet you're on the track

So let this be a warning
For you never never know
Which one of all the boys around
Will be the next to go.

It appears from George's poem that he got the sack and he reckoned Rabbit was behind it. If George did get the sack, it was not because of any lack of competence or through any misdemeanour. It is far more likely it was because of the inability of the station, including us, to tolerate the blurring of the racial divide.

There had already been a long campaign outside our flat earth to give Aboriginal and Torres Strait Islander peoples the right to vote in all state and Commonwealth elections. There was also a campaign to remove the inequality of Indigenous people embedded in the Australian Constitution as far back as 1929. This culminated in the successful May 1967 referendum that gave the Commonwealth government the right to make laws regarding Aboriginal and Torres Strait Islander people and was passed with 90.77 per cent of Australians voting 'Yes', making it the most successful Commonwealth referendum ever.

One important result was that Indigenous people had to receive the same wages as white people, a change that heralded the end of the Aboriginal stock camps. While this had been foreseen, few could have predicted the immediacy of the impact of equal wages on the Aboriginal camps. Suddenly the cattle stations had to meet equal pay and conditions, and they responded with the time-worn solution of mechanisation replacing people. In no time a Cessna was added to the station plant so that cattle could be found more quickly from an eye in the sky. Large trucks moved cattle around the station, taking horses out from the cattle camp to where the mustering started, which cut out three or four hours of riding each day. The cattle were now mustered into steel yards with drafting facilities that had replaced the old bronco yard.

The Aboriginal stockmen went back to the missions as economic refugees, many never to work again. They became grandfathers and fathers to children who had never experienced a male role model in employment. All could have been avoided if there had been transitional arrangements such as a wage subsidy to help both them and the station owners to find a new equilibrium based on equity rather than race.

There is no excuse for the disparity between white and Black in my time, but it could have been reformed differently and with much less lasting damage. Surprisingly, many old Aboriginal ringers look back with some nostalgia to the days when they had skills that were valued. They are passing quickly now, and with them goes their unique history and contribution to the pastoral industry.

I wish I had been different back in 1960 and had taken the trouble to learn what it was like being an Aboriginal ringer and the life that led them to it. I could have enquired about living under the control of the Presbyterian missionaries at Doomadgee, with their strictly supervised life that included singing hymns as the main amusement for girls. All of them were taught that spiritual and material benefits required sacrifice, and this Christian belief might have been indoctrinated into them with the intention of making them more malleable in the face of their great loss.

I might have asked whether the coastal Lardil people from Mornington Island missed the sea and the abundant fish they once caught there, or whether the Aboriginal ringers from the Mornington Mission had mostly been drawn from among those who had been sent there from the mainland. Any possible friendship between us was blocked by the Act and the attitudes that held it in place. A station the size of Augustus holds many Aboriginal artefacts: shield and canoe scars in trees along the river, graves and art in overhangs along Sandy Creek in the Top End. It was all around us, but we wore blinkers and earmuffs.

(Left) My father in the German mounted cavalry and as a forward scout on the Russian front during the First World War. *(Right)* My mother and father in Shanghai, 1935.

Their glory years in Shanghai from 1933–38.

(Left) The three of us seven years apart—Angela, me, Chris. *(Right)* The budding cowboy at Lake Parramatta.

Robbie pushing and me pulling his little sister and my little brother up North Rocks Road past McQueanies shop.

Robbie McCann (left) and me in our tin canoe on the creek below our cave.

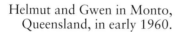

Helmut and Gwen in Monto, Queensland, in early 1960.

Ken Peut on one of the bronco horses with a greenhide lasso at his side ready to pull calves up to the bronco ramp for branding.

The full complement of station vehicles— the camp truck and a landrover— could fit into this shed.

The ringers' quarters showing part of the shower block to the left.

When at the station we rolled our swags out on wire frame beds in the breezeway. On the wall behind Alan Candlish is the Hookey game handed to me by Sam Nugent in memory of Leon.

Joe Clifford, the horsetailer, on Mischief ready to take lunch and our dinner horses out to a predetermined spot to exchange horses for the big drive of cattle back to the camp.

A typical camp. The old Ford truck unpacked, and all the cook's apparel and our food under the fly.

Les Cockerill on the left with King Davy between him and Ken Peut in late 1961. Ralph Tate is sitting on bronco ramp and Joe Clifford, Des Meisenhelter and myself are to the right.

Ken at lunch between branding at the nearby bronco yard and tailing them out on horseback for an hour or so hoping the cows would join up with their calves before nightfall. (PHOTO RALPH TATE)

The only set of full drafting yards were near the station buildings. They were used for making sure all the steers were correctly branded and for dipping them as well as spaying cows, which is what Reg Nissen is doing here.

With Des (right) at the 1961 Burketown races. How I wasted my time. Regrets, I have many and would love to go there now to try and see it as it was then.

Heading out to Fiery with rifles ready in case of an unexpected encounters with buffalo and brumby. I am sitting above the open passenger door. A fresh string of horses have already departed with Joe and Percy.

Ralph Tate ready to lasso a cleanskin calf.

A calf pulled up to the bronco ramp. As soon as the leg ropes are fixed, the lasso is released. The next calf is quickly branded, inoculated and castrated if a male, and the next calf is on its way.

Bert Katter, representing Katter Bros' big store in Cloncurry, did his rounds of the stations with a treasure trove of new moleskins, shirts, hats and a variety of leather horse gear. Reg Nissen made sure we were at the station when he came around.

The ringers' dining room and cook's quarters and kitchen in a slab building at Camboon. It still had two overlapping holes to shoot at any Aboriginal attackers.

JTN Bell drafting his beloved horned Herefords. (PHOTO COURTESY SUE BELL)

The turning wheel of history. Minnie Bell, sister of Barney Joyce, in the slab hut used as a retreat from the attack by the Wulli Wulli people, to whose language group Billy Ivory, standing next to her, probably belonged. (PHOTO COURTESY SUE BELL)

My father at seventy-two and an industrial designer at Amalgamated Wireless Australasia. Me at twenty and at Hawkesbury Agricultural College.

Guaranteed to knock you out. One of the scintillating tutorials by Hawkesbury Agricultural College's vet Norm Jones.

With one of the college Arab mares when back at Hawkesbury in early 1967 as tutor in the beef section.

At the same time I got to know and appreciate Brahman cattle.

The Kienzle family at Kokoda with Bert in the centre, John to his right. Mrs Kienzle in front with Sammy, who lived with them. Young Soccer Kienzle, who accompanied me on our hike up the Kokoda Track, Margaret (Kienzle) and husband John Hardy with their child. (PHOTO BY DIANE KIENZLE)

(Left) At Isurava on the Kokoda Track. Below our guest hut verandah were machine gun shells left from the great battle between Australian and Japanese fighters. I did not touch them but doubt they have survived the later tourists. (Right) At the helm of the beautiful yacht *Enid* on the way to Noumea.

The older I get, the better I used to be. A few rides and a few busters. Great memories.

Three brothers. From right to left, Chris, Helmut and me. Thank goodness we brought along all those water bottles!
(PHOTO ANNE BRECKWOLDT)

At Hilltop in the Bega Valley early 1976. We spent the next thirty-four years getting the house and farm in order.

Proud father of Dan born 1978.

With long-time friend Phillip Hughes after he left Augustus Downs to manage Bulloo Downs in far south-west Queensland.

Counting our cattle on one of my all-time favourite horses. (PHOTO DAMON SMITH)

11

WHITE DREAMING

It was easier to get around Australia by sea, and many ships and sailors of the British navy rocked in the cradle of the infant colony. Phillip Parker King, son of Governor Philip Gidley King, arrived in Port Jackson in September 1817 to complete the charts Matthew Flinders had begun in northern waters in 1802. The Admiralty now wanted to know if there were navigable rivers to populate the interior from the north. The Colonial Office required information on climate, vegetation, fauna, natural resources, and prospect for trade with 'the natives'. During his hydrographic journey, in 1818 King named Port Essington on the Coburg Peninsula after his 'lamented friend' Vice-Admiral Sir William Essington, who commanded British ships during the American War of Independence, the Napoleonic Wars and the French Revolutionary Wars.

Next came Lieutenant John Lort Stokes on board the famed *Beagle*, now being used for charting northern waters under Commander John Clements Wickham, who was often unwell and appointed Lort Stokes as acting Captain. In 1840 Stokes had a crew row him up a big river in the Gulf of Carpentaria that he named the Albert after Queen Victoria's consort. They rowed well past where Burketown sits today before Stokes climbed a muddy bank to view a wide arc of grassland dotted with trees. The following year he was promoted to Captain and he named the area the 'Plains of Promise' in his *Discoveries in Australia*, published in London in 1846, predicting that 'ere long the now level horizon would be broken by a succession of tapering spires rising from the many Christian hamlets that must ultimately stud this country, and pointing through the calm depths of the intensely blue and gloriously blue skies of Tropical Australia, to a still calmer and brighter glorious region beyond'.

The Ganggalida would have watched Captain Stokes and his men and may not have regarded them as entirely strange, but they also knew about muskets. The Ganggalida had been trading with Indo-Malayan seafarers for some thousands of years, as had other northern Aboriginal people. The seafarers came for trepang and traded artifacts for food. Trade included dingo pups, which the seafarers carried as live food. Dingoes have been here for at least 4,000 years, one measure of the length of contact Aboriginal people had with distant races.

Lort's dreaming about villages and churches disregarded the Aboriginal owners and their spiritual beliefs. Just to the south of the Ganggalida were the Mingin, who occupied about 6500 square kilometres on the western side of the Leichhardt River up to the Albert River, including Augustus Downs and Gregory Station. The stations and river had been named after the explorers Leichhardt and Augustus Charles Gregory. European explorers named their 'discoveries' as badges of honour, a right without limits. Aboriginal names were of no importance in their work for a Queen Victoria in faraway Britain.

The Ganggalida and Mingin resisted the white invaders but paid a heavy price as they were 'dispersed', with that euphemism for shooting them gaining tacit government approval. In 1880 the manager of Gregory Station reported that police rounded up Aboriginal people and shot them. Only five years later the manager of Lawn Hill Station reported that police shot more than 100 Aboriginal people in three years; influenza and the 1856 outbreak of yellow fever did the rest. In 1856 a yellow fever epidemic centred on Burketown reduced its population of seventy to fifteen in less than a year, with no person over the age of forty surviving. Today the Mingin are regarded as an extinct race and the Ganggalida speak for that country.

Lort Stokes's idealistic visions were being talked about well before his book was published and heard by Ludwig Leichhardt, a Prussian who arrived in Sydney via London in February 1842. Leichhardt hoped for employment as a government scientist, but what became the Museum of Sydney was then no more than a room in the Central Criminal Courts in Darlinghurst and Governor Gipps decided a gardener was cheaper than a scientist to maintain the rudimentary botanic gardens. Leichhardt turned down teaching work to continue his lone explorations around Sydney, then the Hunter Valley before riding to Moreton Bay, to the edge of exploration and back to Sydney. Leichhardt spent time in the bush with Charley, an Aboriginal companion who would later join his expedition.

Leichhardt heard about a government-funded expedition to Port Essington, which had been suggested as a site for a northern settlement in 1824 but had never progressed beyond being a small military outpost. The government expedition failed to materialise but, not to be thwarted, Leichhardt found sponsors who might benefit from northern riches and staffed his expedition with volunteers. They departed on 1 October 1844 from Jimbour on the Darling Downs, the edge of white occupation at the time. Leichhardt reached the Plains of Promise in the middle of the wet season and his cattle, horses and camels got bogged in flooded black-soil gilgais. They crossed a flooded river that would one day bear his name.

One of his party, John Gilbert, was killed and two members wounded in an attack by Aboriginal men on the night of 28 June 1845. In *The Death of John Gilbert,* B.J. Dalton stated his belief this was meant more as a payback attack, intended to wound rather than to kill. It was probably in response to an unwitting breach of Aboriginal lore by Leich-hardt's party. Roper and Calvert were the two expedition members wounded in the incident that killed Gilbert; they recovered by the time the expedition reached Port Essington on 17 December 1845, almost six months later.

The Leichhardt expeditioners returned to Sydney by boat, arriving on 25 March 1846 to a welcoming crowd after trav-elling around 8000 kilometres and being given up for dead.

Leichhardt made favourable comment on the agricultural potential of the north and his maps showed how to get there.

Inspired by Leichhardt's meticulous diaries, the Colonial Office in London sent Augustus Charles Gregory on an expedition to find out more about this northern wealth. Gregory's diligence and ability as a surveyor at the frontier of pastoralism in Western Australia had attracted the attention of the Colonial Office. He also had had experience in leading a successful expedition to the Gascoyne River.

In August 1855 Gregory's party, which included the scientist Ferdinand von Mueller, sailed from Moreton Bay and the next month reached the Victoria River where it enters the sea in the Joseph Bonaparte Gulf (named by the French explorer Nicholas Baudin in 1803 after the brother of Napoleon). Gregory went inland as far as the Tanami Desert and returned by land via the Flinders and Burdekin rivers. The Flinders had been named after Matthew Flinders by Captain John Clements Wickham when he was captain of the *Beagle* in 1839. Wickham named a big coastal river in honour of himself but, unaware that it had been named the Wickham, Leichhardt named it the Burdekin after one of his sponsors and that name stuck. One as yet unnamed river was crossed by Gregory and he named that in honour of Leichhardt, who had crossed it before him.

Gregory returned to Brisbane, having covered within sixteen months in his west-to-east journey across Northern Australia 3219 kilometres by sea and 8047 kilometres over land. Being a meticulous surveyor, his journal contained a trove of information about the land and water he had crossed. He was less euphoric about the natural resources of this area than some of his predecessors. Gregory was duly awarded the gold medal by the Royal Geographical Society; however, because his expedition was successful and without mishap, it did not attract the same attention as other more dramatic ventures.

One of those was the disappearance of Leichhardt, and in 1858 Gregory led an expedition sponsored by the New South Wales government to search for him. Leichhardt had perished, along with all the other members of his expedition, during his journey across the centre of Australia from the Darling Downs to the Swan River in 1848. Gregory only found traces of Leichhardt and was forced back by drought.

In 1859 Gregory was appointed the first surveyor-general of Queensland, which had just been granted independence from New South Wales by Queen Victoria, on 6 June. Gregory was an unabashed supporter of pastoralism and of any legislation that would enshrine it, so it's not surprising that his contribution would be celebrated by the naming of Augustus Downs Station, its neighbour Gregory Downs Station, and also Gregory, the small settlement within its boundaries.

~

So far the European script for northern Australia had been written by the explorers but it was being closely read by the squatters, always pushing out the edge of the colony wherever there was opportunity.

A most unlikely star performer to act on that script now entered the stage. Oscar John de Satgé had the pedigree, ability, charm and presence to straddle politics and pastoral action. The *Australian Dictionary of Biography* has him born in England on 20 November 1836, whereas Wikipedia has him born on the same date in Lausanne, Switzerland. As this is not a doctoral thesis in history I shall simply rest it at that, with the note that it is just another mysterious aspect of his amazing life.

De Satgé was born into a family that gave him all the benefits of social standing but without the accompanying funds. His father, Ernest Valentine, had the title of Vicomte de Satgé de St Jean bestowed on him by the Duchess of Berry in 1830, but he had been exiled soon thereafter for his role in a royalist revolt. His grandfather on his mother's side was Sherrington Sparkes, the high sheriff of Brecon, Wales. The family was of Catalan origin and, through a lineage to a high-ranking baron, held seigneurial rights to a chateau and its lands in Spain. These rights allowed the signeurs to charge rent for farmland under their control, rather than direct ownership, in return for loyalty to the king. That may have provided the family with enough financial support for them to return to England when their exile was later withdrawn.

Oscar de Satgé received his education at Rugby before departing for Australia at the age of seventeen with his nineteen-year-old brother and arriving in Melbourne in May 1853. He is widely described as being handsome, charming and pleasant company. Fortunately he recorded his Australian experience in a self-published memoir, *Pages from the Journal of a Queensland Squatter,* published in London in 1901.

One of his great talents was name-dropping and his book is a who's who of the times.

Oscar's older brother, Ernest Valentine Léon, headed straight to Brisbane, where he held letters to some of the squatters who had their city residences there. Within a year he was managing Mangola Station on the New England Table-land and he developed a reputation as a horseman of note. He subsequently married into the Tooth brewing family and returned to England, where he became the second Vicomte de Satgé de St Jean.

Meanwhile, Oscar was employed as a clerk to the com-missioner of goldfields in Victoria and travelled to the Ballarat diggings by bush track along which bushrangers relieved people of their gold and sometimes their lives. Letters from Ernest encouraged him to go squatting, and he travelled to Brisbane to 'yield to the fascination of open air and freedom, and so join him'. Oscar then headed south on horseback. When he finally arrived at Mangola, he described the staff there: 'The station staff consists of a chinaman cook, who also acts as a general servant, a stockman and his wife, and a couple of black boys native of Mangola, who could ride anything, and in bush parlance, could track a mosquito.'

Oscar started working as a drover. On one trip to the Dawson River in Queensland he heard of shepherds being killed by Aboriginal people, which led him to the view that 'wild blacks' should never be employed or trusted because they could 'detect weak parts' for attack. He took sheep from Dalby to Victoria and wrote: 'Overlanding promotes restlessness and ambition, so I was soon anxious to get fresh work and applied from Melbourne, to Mr Edmund Lloyd, whose brother had married my cousin, to see if he could put anything my way.'

Mr Lloyd was a member of the Upper House in the New South Wales parliament and a prominent business-man. Queensland was still under the control of New South Wales and Lloyd was able to advance his interests, and he did indeed put something Oscar's way: first as overseer on a property on the Namoi River and then as its manager. In 1859, just five years since beginning his life in the world of the squatter, Oscar was promoted to assistant manager of the Lloyd group of properties in the Namoi region.

In early 1861 Oscar accepted an offer from Gordon Sandeman, who was about to 'be connected to me by marriage' and had previously been the member for the elec-toral district of Moreton, Wide Bay, Burnett and Maranoa in the New South Wales House of Assembly. Oscar and Sandeman became partners in the stocking and development of a large property in the Peak Downs area west of Rock-hampton. This is now part of the Bowen Basin coal-mining area based on Moranbah and Clermont; then it was at the edge of pastoral expansion.

Leichhardt had named the mountain range Peak Range and described the surrounding country as some of the finest in Australia. Ernest soon joined the partnership and they purchased Wolfang Station, named after a peak shaped like the tooth of a wolf. Not long afterwards a station owner, his overseer and his wife and child and nineteen station hands were killed by local Aboriginal people. The only survivors were the station owner's two sons, who were away at boarding school. Sandeman was sympathetic to the Aboriginal people but Oscar said that was too dangerous and approved the retribution applied to those who had murdered the station owner and his staff; he was critical of the murdered pastoralist, believing he had treated Aboriginal people too well.

The squatters of the Ipswich Club, whom Oscar described as the 'cream of squatting in Queensland', were his companions during his frequent visits to Brisbane. They referred to themselves as the 'pure merinos'. They wanted people like them in parliament to protect their interests and Oscar answered their call. He was duly elected to the Upper House of the Queensland parliament to help facilitate the passage of the Pastoral Leases Act 1869, which gave squatters rights of tenure at low rental. To appease opposition to the act it contained a clause that gave the government the right to resume a lease, or part thereof, if this was approved by both houses of parliament. The squatters were not too concerned about this because the majority of members were sympathetic to them.

The passage of the act began a flurry of squatters pegging out country all over Queensland, among whom John Costello was one of the most active. He was the brother-in-law of Patrick ('Patsy') Durack, who founded a celebrated pastoral dynasty as recounted in the classic *Kings in Grass Castles* written by his granddaughter Mary Durack. Costello accompanied Durack on an expansionary journey north that began at Goulburn in New South Wales.

John Costello lived at Kyabra and began creating numerous grass castles for himself. He went west along Cooper Creek, claiming land on the Georgina River that would be called Carandotta, and then north to claim land that included Augustus Downs. When Costello's grandmother complained about him claiming so much land, he replied that it would fulfil all their promises to friends and family. His grandmother replied, 'And what if they've sense enough in their heads to say no to yer kindness.' To which he responded that if they did not want it he would sell the rights to those rushing north in the search for land.

Oscar was also circling the big country. His syndicate purchased the lease of 1295 square kilometres of Coreena on the Barcoo River near Aramac. When this was sold in 1881 for a handy profit of £70,000, his syndicate acquired Carandotta with the incidental, to them, of the attached lease of Augustus Downs. Who it was acquired from and the price of the acquisition I cannot discover, but John Costello was the likely seller for the price of £3000. The de Satgé syndicate invested all of their profits from the Coreena sale into stocking the huge 10,360-square-kilometre Carandotta, purchasing 100,000 sheep, 20,000 cattle and 800 horses. The sale of Wolfang in 1875 for more than £100,000 also funded the stocking of both Carandotta and Augustus Downs.

With a manager in place, Oscar left Australia in 1882 to live at Folkestone in England. He married that year and later had three children, then returned to Australia in 1883, 1888 and 1893 to visit the syndicate properties. It was during his 1888 visit to Carandotta that he made the long trip to Augustus Downs by horse and buggy. He described his visit:

> My stay at Augustus Downs was not long, being sufficient to plan out the work, after inspecting the excellent head of cattle on a tract of closely grassed and abundantly watered country, just one tenth the size of Carandotta, it was a jolly little run, however no waste of country about it, and possessed the very unusual advantage of being watered to its full grazing capacity, not by dams or wells, but by the river and natural lagoons; this gave the run a great advantage of a breeding place, as calves and their mothers never got away too much in this hot part of Queensland.

Augustus and its big neighbours of Lorraine-Tallawanta and Gregory Downs were largely unfenced runs, but natural waters helped keep the branded cattle at home. What Oscar didn't say is that the dependence on natural waters, particularly the Leichhardt River, caused serious land degradation that subsequent owners have been left to deal with.

The big drought of 1892 hit hard. In all, 90,000 sheep and 10,000 cattle perished at Carandotta. As if this was not enough disaster, along came the financial crash. The attempt by banks and city investors to reclaim their excessive funding added to the difficulties faced by pastoralists. Having lost heart and the money that pumped it, the syndicate refused to restock Carandotta but then the banks stepped in. Carandotta and Augustus Downs were resumed by the Bank of New South Wales, its major lender, and sold in 1903 to Sidney

Kidman by the noted stock and station agency Pitt, Son and Badgery Limited. Carandotta may have been managed by Pitt, Son and Badgery on behalf of the bank until a buyer was found or they took on the debt. Later, Kidman took on a partner and Kidman Brody were the owners of Augustus Downs when I arrived there in 1960.

Oscar de Satgé died on 26 September 1906 at the age of seventy-five and left an estate worth just £443, but my research into Carandotta led me to Stephen Long's doctoral thesis on the impact of pastoralism on the Georgina and Diamantina rivers and this put Oscar squarely in the frame— this time as the father of three children by an Aboriginal woman employed on Carandotta. This is quite extraordinary, given his support for the dispersion of the Aboriginal owners of pastoral properties and because there is not even a hint of his second family in Australia in his memoir or in any official accounts of his life.

Those three children have led me to many de Satgés in Australia today. Ruby de Satgé, the daughter of his Aboriginal son Thomas and therefore grandchild of Oscar, became an eloquent writer and activist for Aboriginal rights on pastoral properties. Ruby had clearly inherited his talent for written expression and energy.

A simple search of the residential telephone directory for Queensland comes up with other de Satgés. That, of course, reveals the male line as the females may have taken on other surnames if they married. A long and fascinating phone conversation with Ian de Satgé revealed that the de Satgé family tree is growing; for example, de Satgé's son

Thomas had eight children, including Ruby, and now has great-grandchildren.

~

Today there is an airstrip at Augustus and wings have replaced buggies. The airstrip at Augustus Downs is 6 kilometres away from the station buildings and was built in April 1942 as an advanced operational base military airfield in direct response to the February Japanese bombing of Darwin. This event generated the next big changes at the station as an underground telegraph station, a mess hall, accommodation huts and a telecommunication infrastructure were constructed. There were problems from the start: the surface was too soft to carry a bitumen runway and could not support parked bombers and fighter jets, and the connecting road to the nearest railhead at Dobbyn, 160 kilometres away, was impassable in the wet season.

The people staffing the airstrip lacked a good water supply, because they regarded the Leichhardt River as being contaminated by cattle. Their first operational flight of three Bristol Beaufort bombers, scheduled for 29 October 1942, was reduced to two because the crew of the third came down with what was described as 'dysentery'. A decision was then made to abandon the Augustus Downs base for a replacement near Normanton.

By August 1943 only a few guards remained at the Augustus base to protect the remaining equipment before it was abandoned completely by the RAAF in 1944. In 1946 it was licensed by the Civil Aviation Authority as the airstrip for Augustus Downs Station. All that remains is a long red gravel strip surrounded by grass that was kept low before it merged into silver-grey, broad-leaved eucalypts.

I would soon be drinking water pumped directly from the Leichhardt River to serve the station buildings and staff. None of us ever got sick from it.

12

THE DRY END

'Call the professor,' said Ken as he and Joe engaged in a robust argument around the campfire about whether there was such a thing as a tangerine. Ken said it was bullshit, and if they existed he would have heard about them. No surprise there, given he had never strayed far from Julia Creek and the big stations of the Gulf Country. Joe said he knew about them as a child, which in his case was a long time ago, and there was that certificate lurking in the background.

My academic status was only occasional and applied without sarcasm or mocking, just a factual assessment that I had attended school longer than anyone else. I resolved the tangerine issue in the affirmative and peace resumed around the campfire. My professorship had tight boundaries: spout too much knowledge and you entered the smart-arse class. However, on one occasion I was prepared to test the gap.

A few of my comrades held the unshakeable belief that a goanna bite resulted in the lifelong curse of an erupting putrescent sore at precisely the same spot on the same day of the year for all of your allocated years. Moreover, each subsequent eruption took the exact same number of days to heal as that very first bite. My turn to declare bullshit, but they said that, coming from 'down south', I had no idea what a goanna bite could do.

On a slow Sunday afternoon, I walked up Fiery Creek in search of a suitable goanna; I was out to shoot the smart-arse breeze on this one. I knew from previous chases that I could keep up with a speeding goanna raised high on its two hind legs for less friction. I could gain the advantage when it reached a tree by grabbing its tail just before it climbed out of reach, then it was a simple matter of getting one hand behind its head and the other in front of its flailing rear legs.

I caught the perfect specimen and arrived back at the camp as they were sitting around smoking and watching clothes boil. The goanna was not a monster, but it also was not a midget. I was not so worried about a bite from a large goanna, but there was no first-aid kit in the camp. Truth be known, there was probably no first-aid kit at the station either. A small goanna would not prove anything but provoke derision. My demonstration specimen was about a metre long. Big enough to pass the bullshit test.

With a good dose of showmanship garnished with hubris, demonstrating once again that this acorn had not fallen that far from the oak, I announced that they were about to have their myth destroyed forever. I rolled up my sleeve and let that cranky goanna bite me well and truly on the forearm. It hurt and successfully broke the skin, leaving some saliva and raw teeth marks that soon oozed a bit of blood. There was no contesting that this was a good bite from a decent-sized goanna. It was completely healed in a week or so, and that sort of settled it. There was still the odd 'Yeah, wait until this time next year', to which I replied, 'Remember the date, fellas, because I plan on being here.'

Then something almost got in the way of that plan.

~

By late August I had become a handy ringer. There was no more shouting. I was a fully-fledged part of the team. I had worked hard on my riding. I often jumped on big heifers or young mickey bulls as they got up from the bronco ramp after they'd been branded. With nothing to hang on to I'd stay on for a while before being thrown in the dust. The big benefit was learning balance riding. During one of our stints at the station picking up fresh horses for our next camp, Alan and I asked for Slippery, the aptly named buckjumper, to be drafted off from the station horses and left behind for us to practise on over the weekend. Slippery would buck high into the air, do a twist and come down with a jarring jolt in a totally different direction, then he'd do another twist and go up again. We learned how to ride him. I had found self-esteem in living my cowboy dream and Ken was very much part of it, but it took only a heated moment to nearly kill that relationship and my new-found occupation in the bargain.

We were yarding a big mob of cows and calves in thick dust late in the evening; bellowing cows were accumulating in the rear and breaking away, trying to find their calves.

Chasing them on a horse could be both futile and dangerous because they can suddenly cut in front of your galloping
horse and bring it and you down at speed. There were more
cattle than we could handle. Our horses were sinking under
us as our tempers rose. I was working my section of the
mob when Ken rode directly in front of me to push the same
section of cattle I was working. Without a moment's hesita-
tion or thought about self-preservation, I rode straight up to
him with, 'You go and get fucked, Peut.'

Ken stared directly at me. His eyes were popping out from
under his hat; there was not a metre between his horse and
mine. It was as face to face as you can get while mounted. To
my incredulity, he did not say a single word and simply rode
off to continue yarding the cattle.

I was the one who was fucked. I rode back to the station at
the rear, totally dejected and depressed, with a painful tight-
ness concentrated in my stomach knowing that my days at
Augustus were over. An apology to undo my situation did
not even cross my mind.

I did not go to dinner that night or to breakfast the next
morning; I wanted to avoid facing Ken in front of the others.
I retreated to my empty shared room, where I stayed until
lights out before going to my bed in the breezeway. I expected
the sack and waited in purgatory for the next plane out.

Next morning the other ringers went over to the butcher's
shop to cut up a beast that had been hanging for two days
because it had had the protection of a flyscreen at the station
meat house. I could see them all working harmoniously away
and that made me feel even worse.

Then I saw Fred Nissen, the overseer, crossing the yard and walking straight towards the quarters. I awaited my dismissal. With a squeak of the flyscreen door, followed by the bang of the spring that kept it closed, he stepped into my room and said, 'I hear you told the head stockman to get fucked.'

There was no avoiding that one and I replied in the affirmative.

To which Fred said, 'Well, don't let it happen again.'

And with that, he walked out. No counselling, no admonishment. That was it. All over, just like that.

I picked up my butcher's knife and joined the others cutting up. There was a momentary silence between Ken and me, but not another word was ever said about the incident. I deeply appreciated not being made to apologise and cannot judge what my response would have been if Fred had made that a condition of my continuing employment. I would have complied but felt poorly of myself.

Of course, I could have had a different response to Ken riding in front of me that day and accepted that he did it in a moment of frustration and anxiety about not getting those cattle yarded. Perhaps I was not doing as good a job as I thought I was doing? I could also have raised it with Ken in a quieter moment and maybe even thanked him for helping me out, because both I and my horse were exhausted.

But if I had been capable of those responses at that age then it is highly unlikely that I would have been up there as a ringer on a distant cattle station in the first place. Or is it just another variation of how drive, determination and self-absorption can get a person to a particular destination, but on arrival they're no longer fit for purpose?

Here, there was no culture or system for discussing abrasive issues; there were no human resources managers to train us in conflict resolution. Perhaps Fred had missed his calling. I never found out what transpired between him and Ken.

Sitting above it all, however, the rule that you never rode between a ringer and his position on the herd was in fact highly functional and important. Imagine the mayhem if every time someone thought they could do it better, they just swapped their position by riding in front of whoever was managing it as best they could at the time.

It could be very stressful being at the tip of the wing and taking responsibility for the direction the mob took. Someone might ride up and say to you, 'Do you want a break?' But no one darted in front of another ringer when a mob of cattle was travelling because that way teamwork would be destroyed in an instant and the cattle would move even more slowly, if at all. It was a golden rule: do not ride in front of another ringer doing his job.

Ken would never know that I continued to regard him highly in his ability to walk away from our confrontation, leaving us both with our integrity intact. That started me really liking him, and our working relationship went from strength to strength. The other ringers knew nothing about it and had simply thought my retreat had been through not feeling well. They were correct, but it was not the flu.

~

Towards the end of my year, there were ten horses in my string, with some of them not so quiet. I was getting to think like a horseman without really knowing it. 'Respect' is probably the right word for our relationship with our horses, which went well beyond simply seeing them as a tool for the job of working cattle, and the emphasis on being in control did not represent an ego tussle between man and horse. None of us saw our horses as extensions of ourselves, compensating for inadequacies and turning us into something we were not. We might laugh and tease about gazing at our shadows when on a good-looking horse, but no ringer Narcissus turned into a water lily. I thought about what made a good horse and found it differed little from what I wanted to be: good-looking, smart, quick on my feet, easy to get along with and possessing an ability to anticipate.

It was reasonable to assume that some of the behaviour of your horse related to the way it was thinking and not necessarily what you wanted it to do. However, if a horse baulked we never resorted to some complicated explanation such as: 'This horse just wants to defy me and test me out all the time.' It was never spoken about because anthropomorphism—attributing human behaviour to a horse—never occurred to us. We did not treat our horses as pets, nor did we need substitute children.

The underlying principle was that you were the rider, and it was important that the horse responded to your needs. There was absolutely no reason for us to feel sorry for our horses in any normal work situation as the stockhorses on Augustus led a charmed life 90 per cent of the time. Except for the two months or so they were chosen for a mustering run of camps, they spent the remainder of the year in the big horse paddock with their mates. Care went into keeping their saddlecloths clean and we washed them weekly. In retrospect, our saddlecloths, made of a thin blanket-type material, were the only weakness and sore backs were common. Most of the working horses had a patch or two of white hair behind their withers, indicating they had endured a sore back. Nowadays, a visit to any saddlery reveals a multitude of padded saddlecloths for all occasions.

A saddler visited Augustus every year to counter line the horse hair under each saddle—that is, remove any bumps that would cause sore backs on the horses. During my three years as a ringer I did not encounter a single horse getting badly injured. Some days could be long and hard, and horses got knocked up often enough, but they recovered after their evening drink and a couple of days' spell before their turn came around again. Cruelty was frowned upon; there were no aids except our reins and the occasional use of spurs in the Top End, as I've previously explained.

Without complex theories on horse and ringer psychology, we became sensitive to their individual differences and could subtly adjust the pressure on the reins according to their idiosyncrasies. Some signals—such as ears being pulled back and eyes rolling to show the whites more intensely when you were preparing to mount, and an arched back and stiffness that showed the horse was tight and ready to buck when mounted—are more obvious to the experienced than to the novice. I learned how to respond. If you were getting such signals you had to give the horse a loose rein when you were mounted; if it was tight and humping up you had to have sufficient confidence to ease it away slowly and talk it out of what it was about to do to get you off its back. Sometimes it was possible, sometimes not.

There could often be some fear involved. I tossed and turned in my swag often enough when I knew I was going to have a tough horse in the morning. Not a cold sweating fear but a tense apprehension, which might have been an essential part of dealing with that horse. No one talked about fear, but we knew it was there. A difficult horse might be dodged until someone noticed what you were doing and quietly said: 'Quite a while since I have seen you on Rocky, Roly.' Such subtle social pressure would see that difficult horse taken on at the next camp.

I started the year smoking and ended it quitting. I wanted to abandon Jack's legacy, but I did not realise how hard it would be. I could get through the day, but sitting around the campfire at night and watching the others light up was sheer agony. In the beginning I caved in and asked for a paper and tobacco with the shameless lie that I had run out, but bludging was not a long-term solution and the only way out was not to buy the makings next time we were at the station. A few days turned into a week, then a month went by before the cure began to take hold. I have great empathy for smokers who want to quit; nicotine is a tough boss.

~

Mum had written to me in July to say she would like to come and visit. I put a stop to that idea very quickly in my response to her on 29 July 1960: 'As you can imagine I would very much like to see you and Chris in the September holidays, but it wouldn't be possible where would you stay? I am only a worker on the place. I cant go and ask the manager could you sleep in the "Big House". You couldn't stay in the men's quarters or the blackfellow huts. So I'm afraid it is just not possible. If Chris were old enough he could certainly come up, but not both I'm afraid. Anyhow I shall be home for Christmas so don't worry.'

Then, in late August, not long after my bleary-eyed return from the Gregory Downs races, Reg called me to his office to say he had received a letter from my mother saying that I had been accepted into Hawkesbury Agricultural College. Totally unknown to me, she had put my name down for Hawkesbury when I was a young child after she had heard about it from a neighbour. More surprising was that my four bare passes in the intermediate certificate made me eligible for enrolment. I had absolutely no interest in taking up the Hawkesbury offer, and asked Reg to write back to Mum to say I was perfectly happy here. That is the way I remember it: a perfunctory dismissal of the idea. However, it appears I was much more conciliatory in my own letter to Mum of 20 August 1960:

> Well I suppose you are anxious to hear what I think about going to Hawkesbury college. Mr Nissen had a talk with me about it and both agreed that it would be a very good thing if I went through it. But you realise that it is going to cost a hell of a lot of money and I would not like to have you paying for it all, so what's say I try and get in, not next year

but the year after. By then I should have saved quite a bit of money and you would not have to foot the bill on your own. Anyhow maybe you would write and tell me what you think about the idea. I thank you very much mum for everything you are doing for me down there. And I see that you want me to get ahead in life and be somebody, again I thank you.

My horizon at this time was firmly set on becoming a head stockman, and perhaps one day rising to overseer. I had put limits on myself and could not visualise becoming a manager by jumping the invisible wall I had built around myself. This did not mean I was without enthusiasm and commitment to our daily work. I was like the other ringers who stayed and with whom I worked at Augustus—they had had an incredibly high level of engagement and commitment to their work.

There was something else driving us and it came from within, and it was probably held in place by our competitiveness. Who was the fastest on foot in the bronco yard? Who was the best horseman? Who was the person you wanted to be with when things got tough? There was no need for individual performance targets or personal reviews—we lived a full-time 360-degree performance review with, 'Eat quick, shit quick and ride a buckjumper, and you will get a job on any cattle station' being the favoured yardstick.

Remember, there were no shes present then. None graced our camp, and they resided in missed opportunities and fantasies. We were there to work. Play was as scarce as the time allowed for it, and all fun was embedded in work. Personal bonds developed, but they were limited to getting on well to work in harmony. Tempers might flare and harsh words spoken, but they had to be quickly forgotten sitting around a campfire together with nowhere to run or hide behind non-speakies.

I replied to a letter from Holm on 14 November 1960 in which he suggested he could find a mate for me to spend time with during the Christmas break. What the fuck was he thinking? Getting me a mate would be about the last thing in the world I would want from Holm.

I look at my reply now and see that it was brimful of passive aggression. He would have hated my language and attitude; after addressing him as 'Howdy pardner' I followed up with:

Up here everything is going fine, all the cattle work is finished now, as its just too hot to work cattle and horses. All we do now is fencing, yard building, rail and post cutting and miscellaneous odd jobs. The other day we put up 3 miles of fence along the bullock paddock boundary. All the blokes (including me of course) are starting to make preparations for leaving the mulga and hitting the 'Big Smoke'. I understand your very good and kind intentions of selecting me a mate for my holiday. I really appreciate it, but maybe if I saw her first before making a move. I should have £180 quid by the time I toss in the towel here, should be able to have a good time on that.

We arose at 4 am during this hot end of the year and did our fencing or yard repairs in the early morning cool. Then we sat out the heat of the day in the shade before another mid-afternoon to late-evening shift in which I added using a crosscut saw, adze and hand augur to my skill set. Pull the saw, don't push it. There was still some cattle work that involved moving perishing cattle to new water that was beyond their normal walking pattern. Cattle died in many long dry seasons; this was one way the stocking rate adjusted to the country and its management or lack thereof!

Occasionally there was some brumby running on Augustus, when they were skeleton poor at the end of the dry and could be run for a while by Reg in his Land Rover as they emerged from the river weighed down by a bellyful of water. We took over on our horses when the brumbies tired and ran them along a fence to the Boundary Camp horse paddock. Once the brumbies had mated up with our station horses they could be run into the horse yards along with them as coachers.

All this effort only ever produced a few horses suitable for breaking in, and the stallions and older mares among the brumbies were shot in the yard set up for their capture and dragged away. Augustus Downs had plenty of working horses it bred from smaller thoroughbred sires selected for their conformation; the many brumbies were not seen as recruitments and elicited no sentimentality, being simply regarded as feral animals.

Cattle at this drier end of the dry would perish if they stuck to the same waterhole and it went dry. It was a way the land took a hand in controlling the stocking rate; management did the rest. Doing nothing is also management, and there was plenty not done.

Sometimes a group of cattle in a mob we were mustering would separate out and paw at the bony skeleton of a long-dead beast. A couple would often pick up a bone in their mouths and carry them along, chewing it and sucking on it all the while. I asked Reg why they did this and he said it was probably for fun. No concept of mineral deficiency entered our lexicon, and neither did weaning. A calf on its mum's teat for two years kept her in anoestrus. Biennial calving kept numbers low, along with profitability. But there you go, it was another way that the land exerted its influence.

~

There were only two seasons for us—the wet and the dry. The latter was when the mustering and branding took place and the wet was when ringers took their long, unpaid break. A very different seasonal structure to the original Mingin, who would have known seven or eight seasons, all identified by subtle changes in the weather, the wild animal migration and behaviour patterns, and the differing availability of edible plants and their fruits and seeds.

Cultural relevance writes the calendars and seasons. Ours was determined by grass and water for horses and cattle. We ate beef, canned fruit and sacks of potatoes, pumpkins and onions that came on trucks, so the more complex natural cycles passed us by.

There were, however, signs that the dry was coming to an end. By the middle of October, the days were getting longer and hotter. Waterholes were drying up and cattle were getting weaker as the last wet season grass was consumed.

They were getting bogged as they tried to reach the remaining puddles in the middle of lagoons or along creeks. All the country along the Leichhardt River was eaten out, leaving it exposed for the wet season rains to erode it some more.

Large freshwater crocodiles inhabited all the rivers and creeks, and we swam among them without any concern. The falls that divided the lower reaches of saltwater from the freshwater frontage of the Leichhardt River at Augustus were only about 30 kilometres downstream. This would not have been an impediment to the large estuarine crocodiles and our safety was partly a result of them being hunted to endangered status. The freshwater Johnstone's crocodile did not attract hunters during my time because of the much greater value of the skin of the estuarine species. That would change. Without estuarine crocodiles to hunt, the freshwater crocodiles met the same fate until they too became a protected species.

Sitting in the shade of a tree on the banks of the Leichhardt in that hot summer with a mob of cattle that would not be moved until the cool of late afternoon, I entertained myself by annoying freshwater crocodiles that had crowded into the remaining waterholes while waiting for the wet. Although muddy and without any visibility, I could land a clump of cracked riverbed on a crocodile by following its ripple along the turgid surface. A hit would have it thrash about, revealing its considerable size.

Tired of my pointless game, I joined the others and we sat in the shade while we took turns in holding the fifty or sixty head of poor and skeletal cattle that would have perished without the move and may well have done so at their new location if the wet was late or failed. In the ensuing peace, the crocodiles I had annoyed took the opportunity to vacate their waterhole and cross the dry riverbed to the next waterhole to avoid the clod thrower.

Running down, I grabbed a 2-metre freshwater crocodile by the tail. In the same manner as holding a cleanskin bull and hoping it could not reach far enough around to horn me, I held this crocodile along its tail to prevent it biting me. All my entreaties to the others to take its tail so I could subdue it further by taking it behind the front legs failed. I was left with this writhing crocodile while the ringers under the shade of a tree laughed themselves silly at my predicament. Fortunately, the crocodile was more intent on escaping than doing me damage and took off to a new waterhole once I let go.

The end of the year came quickly. We were all paid out and ready to fulfil our little dreams during the wet season break. Only Joe stayed, while we left by plane and car to destinations from Cairns to Sydney and places in between.

13

THE RETURN

It was the sticky end of the monsoon and a foreign land when we got back for the year ahead. Still hot, but now humid. Any memory of starving cattle on empty waterholes was buried under a sea of long grass. Fat cattle grazed long green Mitchell and Flinders grasses that had been so eaten down in the dry you would have sworn they were dead. The gilgais, the small depressions in the black-soil downs, were full of water and Nardoo, the floating fern whose rhizomes lay buried during the dry.

Last November's 'get them through until the rains' was now redundant. Aboriginal people had traditionally hunted native animals living on grass and gathered its seed. Now cattle consumed that grass and we hunted them on horseback. We were modern-day nomads, looking for grass and hoping for good seasons. With the big stations having almost no internal fencing, it meant the cattle could chase storms for new growth.

My six weeks in Sydney had not amounted to anything much, yet I was consumed by loneliness on the long rail journey back to Augustus in late January 1961. No amount of self-talk would make it go away; it was only when I got back among the ringers that I blended back into who I was before the break.

Behind my time away stood a mother and father growing older, a younger brother who had become a stranger to me and a sister with children of her own. Holm was now sixty-eight and had lost his job at the university on reaching the compulsory retirement age of sixty-five. He simply put his age back five years and got a job as an industrial designer at AWA, where he designed the first Echo brand of television they produced. It was a time of full employment and there was no demand for birth certificates.

His beloved garden was failing, and only nostalgia and those rocks we'd collected so long ago kept it intact. Holm was spending his time in a very basic study he'd built beside the house on a slab that was once destined to become a more commodious retreat. His dreams for the rest of the house had perished from his weariness. The roof had not been painted for years, and its one coat of blue had turned to rust. He took solitary holidays on Lord Howe Island. My parents lived separate lives under the same roof. Mum was immersed in lapidary, her latest business venture; she polished bits of agate in a tumble box and hung them on leather necklaces. She worked at night and on weekends at a nursing home for the aged in Carlingford.

Ken confided that he did not get down south to see his sister in Brisbane and had left a year's wages in a pub at

Cloncurry. Apart from that, we did not speak of or ask about what had transpired during our long break. We chorused that Augustus was a good place to work, because we could sign off at the end of the dry and be confident of returning to a job and signing on again.

We were so unworldly, so trusting, we were unaware that by signing us off and then re-hiring us Kidman Brody avoided long service leave, accumulated annual leave, sick leave and the other benefits that went with continuous employment. On the other hand, Reg always paid the white ringers above their age award once they had the skills he valued, and I was about to benefit from that.

Reg called me into his office one afternoon and said I was being promoted into the eighteen- to twenty-one-year-old wage bracket. Barely six weeks later he called me in again and said he had thought it over and would promote me to the full adult wage. At barely seventeen, I loved the recognition as much as the extra wages. Ken would have been a big part of that promotion so he had not dwelt on our differences the year before.

The black-soil downs began drying out enough for mustering. Young horses were broken in, and those with a buck or two in them were given a ride. I slipped easily into the part and soon accumulated sixteen horses in my team.

~

There were three main excuses for taking a break: the Gregory Downs races, Normanton races and Burketown races. You can detect the incredible variety in that. In April Ken, the only one of us who went to the Normanton races, came back with two new ringers. 'Blue' McDermott, with red hair that made his nickname obligatory, was tall, quiet and competent. Ray Davis was stocky and eager to please and talked as if he knew it all, but underneath that lay a try-hard desire to be accepted.

We had mustered a big mob of cattle and held them against a fence around the horse paddock at Dinner Camp Bore while we campdrafted out the steers. There was no weaning, so steers still attached to their mums might be two years of age. During last year's muster they were probably still sucking her teats, which had kept her from going into calf again. That was the basic reason Augustus at that time would have been lucky to have a 45 per cent calving rate. So much of the campdrafting out of the steers we did on horse-back was in fact weaning.

Ken was in the mob doing the drafting and brought a young steer to the face that had just been separated from its mother. I ducked in behind this reluctant steer and drove it on horseback over to the mob of steers nearby that had already been drafted out and were being held by Old Davy and Joe. Then I returned to the face of the cattle to resume my position.

No sooner had the steer been left with Old Davy and Joe than he broke from the steers they were holding to get back to his mum in the main mob. They could not chase him because holding those flighty young steers that had already been drafted out required their full attention. Once again Ken drafted the same steer out. Alan took it over to the other mob of steers and returned to take up his position, but the recalcitrant steer was back at about the same time as him.

Next time it was drafted out we stopped proceedings to make sure it was held securely with the other steers, but instead of staying put, this time the steer took off in the other direction towards a thin line of timber, which is where it could probably last remember a quiet time without this troubling confusion. It was, however, getting tired and cranky and slobbering at the mouth.

Ken was not quite slobbering at the mouth, but he was equally cranky when he said, 'I've had a gutful of this bastard. Let's throw him and take his horns off. That'll stop his farting in church.' He galloped after the steer with me and Ray behind him. At close to full gallop, Ken leaned over and grabbed the steer's tail near its base and then let it slip though his hand until he held the very tip. At full speed, he changed the direction of his horse at a sharp angle, and the leverage and his momentum resulted in the steer falling and rolling over. I had anticipated this and, following behind Ken at just the right distance, I jumped off my horse and lifted the steer's upper hind leg high so it was immobilised. Ken rode back, dismounted and constrained both hind legs of the steer with a set of dinner hobbles he wore as a second belt.

Ken drew his horn saw out from its long pouch, which extended under his saddle's flaps. I held the steer's head for Ken to saw off its horns. The steer thrashed around, making it difficult for him, but it would only have taken a moment longer for it to be held more securely. Meanwhile Ray, trying to do some good, had picked up a thick, short and heavy dead branch at the base of a nearby coolabah to whack the steer over the head and induce it into a more compliant frame of mind.

Trouble is, it was Ray's plan and not ours. Ken was not expecting this form of bovine anaesthesia. Ray bought down the thick, stubby branch with a mighty wallop just as Ken was putting his hand on the end of its horn to get a better grip. The piece of wood, powered by Ray's desperation to be doing good, came down on Ken's hand with an ugly cracking sound. Ken held up his right hand to show three smashed and broken fingers with the bones protruding. I stood wide-eyed, waiting for the world to explode. Ken simply looked at his hand then looked at Ray and said, 'Well, Ray, you have really done it this time.'

Ken remounted and rode a kilometre to camp before being driven by Ralph to the station in the camp truck. Ken had to wait untreated and in great pain all night until the flying doctor arrived the next morning. He was flown to Cloncurry Hospital, and it was three weeks before he returned with his hand still in plaster. In the meantime, both Ray and Blue had gone.

~

There was a sort of sieve operating in finding men who fitted our camp. But the sieve either got clogged or was too fine, and I suspect that Ken determined who got through either by decision or default. An Australian Workers' Union representative called in when we were at the station and talked about the need to improve conditions and wages in the pastoral industry. We were polite but uninterested as it fell so far outside the narrow lens of our experience, and needs for that matter. We felt we were treated well with food and wages and that being a 'good man' was an end in itself. Curious, because we were all transients in the end.

Being a good man did have an ethical component, but that was only part of it. Not taking any shit from anyone could make that a fine balance. Being a good man also included being able to ride a rough horse. Holding your own ground in any aspect of the work and taking risks without complaint were also expected of a good man. We had to be able to live and work together in an intense environment which had a pervasive capacity to generate conflict.

One new ringer met most of the criteria but there was a conflict that defied resolution. Bert Quade arrived at Augustus fresh from the cane fields of Mossman near Cairns. He was of average height, solid and strong, and had a slight limp from a motorbike accident that, strangely enough, accentuated the aura of toughness he liked to portray. His most lively conversations centred around all the fights he had won over the years. I can't remember whether I believed him or humoured him. But he was competent and well enough liked.

None of us ever found out what happened between him and Ken. There was talk that it started with Ken ticking Bert off for coming to the dinner table without a wash. Ken was a wash enforcer. Whatever was said must have simmered in Bert until it boiled over. The first thing we heard of it was that Bert would be on the next plane out, but not before, as Bert told us many times, he 'belted the shit' out of Ken.

No amount of Fred Nissen's mediation would have resolved this one. Ken and Bert were evenly matched and here was a bare-knuckle light–heavyweight duel in the offing. Since we were merely bystanders in the duel it did promise an element of entertainment that would make good campfire conversations for years to come wherever we went. But the rumble in the grasslands never came about. Bert's fight was in his head, and he went quietly on the next plane out.

A good man who did not last was Kevin Weedon. He was small and neat, strong, competent and self-contained. He and I were at the tail, driving a big mob of cows and calves that had dug their hooves in. Kevin was contributing, but in a much less energetic way than me. That evening he came up to me in the camp and said: 'I could see by the way you were looking at me that you thought I was being lazy. It is not that at all, Roly. I just have a different way of working cattle than you blokes. I was brought up to work cattle differently.' Kevin resigned soon after and I never saw him again, but his words never left me and many years later I would put his way of doing things into practice.

Another ringer came to take Kevin's place and immediately acquired the name of Split the Breeze because of his obvious lack of speed. He also had a bad case of eczema, and that may have been part of the reason his nickname was applied with such sufficient force that it helped him make the decision to leave within a month. Ken was probably behind that too.

It was about half way through the year that I asked Ken and Reg if they would be prepared to take on a schoolfriend of mine by the name of Des Meisenhelter. Now there is a

German name for you but a more Aussie family you could not meet. Des's father would even join us down at the Northern Hotel at Northmead during that long summer break of mine, something Holm would never do even if you tried to pay him. I was able to shield Des from the shouting and help him through those few first months. Nothing could save him from the hilarity of his description of losing cattle in 'the ravines', which were, of course, the eroded breakaways that led out from the river.

Des and I would roll out our swags next to each other and spend time discussing the fate of the north if Australians failed to develop it. In truth we were not far in front of Rabbit's predictive skills. We came up with all sorts of bullshit such as that if Australia failed to develop the north then the 'yellow peril' would inevitably exercise the option. Neither of us, nor anyone else in the camp for that matter, predicted the mining boom, the beef roads, the technological revolution with its planes, helicopters and satellite imagery all in the wider sweep of contemporary mechanisation, and the changes for Aboriginal ringers. Futurologists we were not, and our effort would put us to sleep.

Des woke up from one such slumber screaming in pain at having been bitten by a swag invader. I had no sympathy for him at all and advised him to get back to sleep lest his noise woke everyone. Next night it was my turn. I was bitten on the neck and it was excruciatingly painful. I pulled out a small torch I carried in my swag and found the culprit, a giant centipede at least 15 centimetres long. I flicked it out into the dark and tried to get back to sleep, but rest evaded me for some hours. That is the only time in my two years of swag dwelling that something with a nasty bite got in.

Ian Varidel joined us in the middle of the year. He was a great talker and told yarns about his time droving on the famed Murranji Track in the Northern Territory. He embellished his stories with descriptions of kangaroos 'bouncing off trucks' and killed in numbers where the track intersects with the Buchanan Highway. The only truck we knew was the old Ford that serviced the camp and there were very few kangaroos on Augustus, these being the sparsely distributed Antilopine kangaroo that actually belong to the Wallaroo family. Part of their scarcity on Augustus would have been dingo predation. With that being the extent of our knowledge of northern Australian macropods, we thought Ian's stories were grossly exaggerated. It was enough for us to change his name from Ian to Murranji.

Murranji was allocated a horse called Flossie. She was very difficult to saddle and stretched his patience beyond breaking point. He ranted, raved and swore at Flossie, who remained totally unimpressed and continued in a world of her own. He also had to mount her quickly as she would take off the moment his feet left the ground. Whenever Murranji could no longer dodge Flossie we all knew there would be an entertaining delay to the day. We would get our horses saddled, mount and leave the yard to wait for him, and our mock impatience only got Murranji more keyed up. Flossie would throw the saddle before he could do up the girth or buck before he could get it tightened with the saddle rolling under her belly where she lashed at it with a well-aimed 'cow

kicks'. It would tip Murranji right over the edge into a spectacular tantrum. 'You are a fucking bitch of a horse, Flossie,
and I hate the fucking sight of you.'

Murranji had some limitations as a horseman because he
had taken it up later than most of us, but there were no limits
to his personality and ability to fit in with everyone. He was
well put together and dressed every part the ringer, working
hard and telling his stories around the campfire.

~

Superficial changes to us, all those come and gone. We were
busy at least six days a week and there was always pressure
to finish at least three mustering cycles a year. Ken carried
most of that pressure, and it was no doubt the reason we
so often ended up with such big mobs at the end of the day.
Smaller mobs meant more days, and more days meant more
wages. Or more ringers, but they both had the same impact
on that very shallow bottom line.

One little break occurred when Bert Katter of Katter
Bros in Cloncurry did his run of the Gulf stations in a truck
converted into a clothing and saddlery store. We simply called
him the 'hawker', and Reg Nissen would make sure we were
at the station when he made his annual visit. It was a major
event and we restocked on clothing, personal saddlery such as
new quartpots as well as knives, belts and other accessories.

Over fifty years later I was standing in the queue at the
supermarket in Kingston, Canberra when I noticed the Hon.
Bob Katter, Member for Kennedy, one step ahead of me.
I introduced myself to the MP and told him how much I'd

appreciated his uncle's hawker run and calling in at Augustus. This time it was Katter who declared bullshit (it seems as though there is a theme here). I assured him without success that this was not the case, and when that failed I said that I had photos to prove it—to which Katter said: 'All right then, make an appointment to see me at Parliament House and show me the photos.' This I did, and I arrived with my photo album. On seeing it, his personal assistant rolled her eyes, as if this sort of thing was not uncommon with her boss, and ushered me in.

'Well, you are right, I did not know that,' said the Honourable MP, then he started to talk a lot about northern Australia. I was conscious of his time and asked how long he had for our appointment, to which he replied that he had about twenty minutes. An hour later, we were still talking . . . I should say, he was talking. Katter told me that he was going to start a large cattle and cropping venture with a syndicate in northern Australia and I would make an ideal manager for it. I replied that I would be interested and could he please email me the position description and conditions of employment. It never arrived.

~

My fondness for reptiles and wildlife in general provided an opportunity for my fellow ringers to play a joke on me. It was my turn to get the horses in for an afternoon of shoeing before we headed up to the Twelve Mile. While I was away, they'd killed a very large Western Brown snake that had innocently entered the camp. Too far north to be an inland taipan, which it resembles, it is a highly venomous snake and lethal in such a distant location. They coiled it up under a bush in a very lifelike position with its mortal wounds well concealed. Upon my return they feigned surprise at suddenly seeing the venomous monster neatly curled up, ready to spread death.

I recommended leaving it alone and it would soon leave of its own accord. My workmates knew this would involve a miracle, so I was asked with great sincerity to demonstrate how to catch and relocate a venomous reptile. I took them through the steps they should follow and proceeded to cut and size a forked stick to control the head of the snake as a precautionary step before taking it by the tail and releasing it some distance from the camp. I explained how this species is highly agile and so large that I would also use the stick to keep it away from my body if it lashed up too high.

Sneaking up quietly to place the forked stick behind the snake's head, I discovered their ruse. I had to live with their hilarity as they told and retold that incident for at least the next two months with multiple variations of 'Please teach us how to catch snakes again, Roly'.

Wildlife was abundant. Riding along, I would catch Black-headed pythons on branches without dismounting. My childhood fantasy about keeping pythons, and especially a baby crocodile, was right there on my doorstep. I caught a young crocodile that gave me such a sharp and deep bite on the finger that it seemed to bleed for hours. With nowhere to keep the crocodile, I released it straight away.

On camp we ate our evening meals, sat around for a while and then went to our swags. The cook extinguished the carbide light. Dingoes howled in the dark distance and cattle bellowed in the holding paddock as cows searched for their calves, still separated by the afternoon muster. The night horse neighed for its mates. Stars blazed in the cloudless, cold dry-season nights. The Milky Way was packed so bright and tight it paved a highway across the sky. But we never marvelled at any of this or shared the moment. We were not wonderment people.

14

THE SACKING OF JOE

There were no speeches, no drinks, no party at the station, no fond farewells when Reg Nissen retired on 30 June 1961. One day he was there, the next he was gone. Ralph decided to leave at the same time, and I cannot remember saying goodbye to him either. Neither were we part of any handover to Les Briggs, the new manager, because we were camped at Fiery and were shoeing horses in readiness for the Top End.

Briggs drove out and introduced himself with attitude. He was short and sandy-haired under a hat unlike the ones we wore. It was smaller than ours, and it set him immediately apart as a manager from another region rather than as a northern ringer who had made the transition.

Indeed, I found out from his son Gary many years later that Briggs had been working for a machinery company in Brisbane when a grader was required in Clermont, a distance just short of 1000 kilometres away. There being no suitable semitrailer at that time to carry such a large item, Briggs volunteered to drive it to Clermont. During this trip he met the owners of Elgin Station; they offered him a job and he became an overseer. After only a year or two at that, the owners recommended him for the position as manager of Augustus Downs. He was very different to Reg and we knew it within days.

Briggs wanted to put his brand on Augustus. When he arrived at Fiery, he offered to take us to the Gregory pub for an evening drink. Any visit to Gregory had previously been reserved for a once-yearly visit to the races. We had never even discussed slipping over to Gregory in the old Ford; the dry status of Augustus had always been a barrier to any contemplation of having a beer at the local.

In the gathering dust, weary from a day's shoeing horses, it was two in the front with him and the rest of us white ringers in the back as we set off for the Gregory pub about 60 kilometres away. What a pleasant surprise—and during the week into the bargain. The Aboriginal ringers didn't get a ticket. Totally unaccustomed to alcohol under such circumstances and making the best of the occasion, we got hopelessly drunk. I don't remember a single thing about that night, and any possible memory was obliterated by shoeing horses next day with an awful hangover. Carrying my head above a stomach that seethed was no way to enjoy the job at hand, but shoe horses I did in the open yard at Fiery, without shade or shelter on a bright and sunny dry-season day. Ken said his mouth felt like the bottom of a pigeon cage.

Joe had made a mess of himself and failed to emerge from his swag for breakfast. He was not missed because Mischief, his mare, did not need shoes for her job carrying the horse-tailer and Joe could not shoe anyway, but when he did rise Briggs sacked him on the spot. We didn't witness this because we were up in the yards, but when I saw Joe's face it showed the great loss of his home at Augustus for the past sixteen years. When it came to supporting Joe, we lacked both word and action; the god manager had decided that Joe was not to be included in his vision of Augustus heaven. Paradise was for the competent.

For all we knew, Briggs might have been sent to Augustus to kick heads and make some changes, but we didn't consider this because management decisions were totally outside our realm. There was no one with any authority to advocate for Joe because Fred had resigned when Reg retired. For all we knew, Fred may have applied for the position of manager on the retirement of his father and his application for the position had failed.

We had neither the confidence nor the initiative to take a stand over the sacking of Joe. Despite our strong physical appearances, we were either less secure than we thought or we simply didn't care enough. I look back and see what a totally unformed individual I was. The time would come when colleagues were shown the door because their billable hours did not meet the company criteria, but I didn't offer to walk with them and neither did anyone accompany me when it was my turn.

As it happened, I need not have worried too much about the sacking of Joe. I learned only very recently that he found a position almost immediately on Floraville, a large station only about 100 kilometres from Augustus. It was owned by Les Huddy, who was also a drover; he frequently called in at Augustus when he was returning with his truckload of horses after delivering cattle to Kajabbi. Huddy was extremely popular among us ringers. He camped with us and spoke like us. Incredibly, in 1969 after eight years at Floraville, Joe returned to Augustus as a grader driver when a new manager replaced Briggs. That lasted a couple of years before Joe moved back to Floraville.

The next time I encountered Briggs was when he joined us killing a beast. I was busy skinning the recently shot bullock and Briggs said, 'Hand me that knife.' He wanted to show that he could mix it with us so I handed him my precious personal butcher's knife and tried to make myself look busy by placing cuts of meat on the back of the truck.

After a while I asked Briggs, 'Could I please have my knife back?'

He said, 'Whose knife?'

With some reserve I said, 'My knife,' to which he repeated himself by saying, 'Whose knife?'

It then dawned on me that he had turned this into a territorial dispute. He believed the knife belonged to the station and I had no right to refer to it as 'my knife'. What Briggs did not know was that it was part of our culture to buy a personal butcher's knife. We would spend hours honing them, holding them dead flat on the sharpening stone so the blade never developed a shoulder that would blunt quickly. I still have that knife, protected in the same leather sheath I made then to keep it sharp.

When Briggs realised his error, he handed the knife back. It was a minor incident but, together with the sacking of Joe, it created a gap between him and me that took a while to heal. It did heal, because I benefited from another of his changes.

After Joe went, the next to go was Ken. Once again, I cannot remember any goodbye. This departure may have been stitched up by Briggs well in advance because, within a few days, Ken was replaced by Les Cockerill from Lorraine Station next door. Les came with a reputation: he had worked at Augustus some years earlier when Reg was the manager and was known as the only person to have ridden Angel, the aptly named buckjumper that had thrown all comers. It was said she would buck high and come down with a low and unpredictable twist, but any pressure on her reins would make her rear over. Cockerill rode Angel with a loose rein, relying totally on balance.

I had met Les in my first year at Augustus, when he 'tended' the muster at Disraeli Camp in his position as head stockman at Tallawanta outstation on Lorraine. 'Tended' is a corruption of 'attended' and refers to when a neighbouring station sends a ringer to assist a next-door muster and bring back any cattle with their earmark. I had been sent over to Nardoo with my gear on a packhorse to tend one of their musters earlier that year.

At that Disraeli tender, I could see that Les had a special relationship with Old Davy. I took a photo then of Old Davy leaning against Les with his arm around his shoulder, which was unusual for Black and white ringers at the time.

Les Cockerill had charisma stamped all over him. On the shorter side of medium height and strong in a loose, lean way, he carried himself with an easy self-confidence and a don't-mess-with-me attitude. No one ever thought about messing with him anyway because he was instantly popular and respected, and his right to be head stockman was beyond challenge. Good at everything, he told great stories. He was another of those men whose raw intelligence shone through their lack of formal education. He was about to demonstrate just how good he was.

He took over Ken's string of horses. Among them was Girlie, a buckjumper of considerable skill that had dumped Ken unceremoniously in the mud at Goose Lagoon on one memorable occasion. That day, we had been mustering the Spayed Cow Paddock and had stopped to give our horses a drink. We rode the horses out knee-deep beyond the fringe of flowering water lilies in shallow mud stirred by our entry. Something must have triggered Girlie, because in one almighty buck she landed the unsuspecting Ken flat on his back in the water. One of us caught Girlie while Ken trudged out, soaking wet, with his riding boots and leggings thick with black mud. We remained silent, knowing that it could easily happen to us. Ken had avoided riding Girlie ever after.

Les reviewed his team as they were drafted through the station round yard before heading out from Fiery and selected Girlie among his team as soon as he heard she was a difficult horse. It seems like it was part of his plan. A few of the ringers said to Les that Girlie was unsuitable as a dinner horse. It was a long time since she'd been ridden and she could really buck, so how was he going to catch her and get on her out in the open? You should take her as a morning horse, it was suggested to him, and ride her first here in the yards and maybe select a quieter dinner horse that could be caught in the open, as we all did. Les simply ignored us, and we knew there was no point in pressing it any further.

With Joe gone, Percy, one of the Aboriginal ringers, had become the horsetailer. He delivered Girlie among the other dinner horses to a waterhole about 5 kilometres down Fiery Creek. After a typically relaxed lunch, Les rigged up a small barrier between three trees using the green-hide ropes that we carried in our pack saddles should they be required for occasions when a dinner horse was difficult to catch. We coaxed Girlie and a couple of other horses into this crude barrier and Les moved quietly among them before he caught her with ease and had a bridle on her in moments.

Already mounted, we watched with anticipation for a display of Les's riding skills on a buckjumper, but our curiosity turned to awe when he saddled Girlie without any resistance from her. We had expected her to buck and throw the saddle as the girth was tightened and the crupper went under her tail, but Les just reined her up, mounted and rode off. Girlie was tight and humped up once or twice. With any encouragement she would have turned it on, but Les simply talked her out of it and rode her with a loose rein that was brought a bit taut now and then just to let her know he was there. He rode her all afternoon without any problem but, most impressively of all, he did not talk about it.

The term 'horse whisperer' was yet to arrive, but I suspect Les was a natural. He certainly put on a display, one that I have never forgotten. Professionals make it look easy; the best display of all is a quiet inner confidence.

Les's ability to handle wild cattle matched his horsemanship. In the Top End he always went out wearing three bull straps. On more than one occasion he took off after a group of scrubbers and then rode back to the coachers, having thrown three of them. He could always remember where they were.

I could not get enough of his stories about Glenhaughton Station, where the scrub was so thick you could barely ride through it and mustering involved chasing scrubbers every day. Here he was talking about the last of the big stations in the Brigalow Belt. Les also talked about Camboon Station, near Theodore, owned by the Bell family. Patriarch JTN Bell had an interest in breeding good horses. I listened intently to Les's stories and was influenced by them, ultimately making up my mind to leave Augustus and get a job on Camboon Station. I didn't know the meaning of mentor, but he was one in that early part of my working life.

Briggs decided that Augustus was running low on working horses and that they would be supplemented by purchasing some unbroken horses from Gregory Downs. Fortunately for me, Les asked me to be his horsebreaker's offsider and I was thrilled to have been chosen. He and I rode the 60 kilometres from Fiery to Gregory Downs and viewed the horses.

There was no possibility of rejecting them, even though we could see they were mostly well over the optimum age of two years. They were giants, big and strong four- and five-year-olds, the offspring of a tall thoroughbred station stallion. We reckoned they were being sold because they'd missed being broken in; Gregory Downs Station would have been very pleased to be rid of them. I was glad it was Les in charge of getting them home and breaking them in, because I was already daunted by their size and had a strong inkling of what lay ahead.

The unbroken horses were let out of the yards at Gregory Downs Station, and they galloped for the first two kilometres before we could slow them a little as we approached the river. The Gregory River is a crystal-clear stream fed by springs at its rocky source in the same ranges as those around Disraeli Camp, and is less affected by the wet and dry. The clear and constant flow supports rich tropical vegetation along its banks with a distinct row of pandanus very like the Leichhardt. At the time we crossed the Gregory River with our mob of unbroken horses it was a base camp for Mount Isa miners who had been displaced by the long strike of 1961 over impending legislation that threatened their contract bonuses.

The contrast between the highly unionised miners on strike and us ringers, working six days a week from dawn until dark under dangerous conditions, totally passed me by. Ringers were widely scattered and moved between stations so frequently that any common interest, expressed in mass meetings and collective bargaining, would have been very difficult to achieve even if it was not impeded by our indifference.

As we had crossed the Gregory, the horses burst over the farther bank and galloped through the miners' tents, caravans and makeshift shelters. People were running to safety behind a tree and yelling at us to control our horses, not realising we were exercising as much control as we could. Cameras were out and I had an audience at last, but alas it was over in minutes.

We finally arrived back at the station after two camps along the way, at Fiery and Dinner Camp Bore, and we started breaking them in. Each horse was broken in within two days and handed to a ringer on the fourth day regardless of what success we had had in making them manageable.

First day, tying it up and bagging down. Second day, in mouthing gear and saddle then driving in reins from behind and mounting and riding later in the day. Neither of us got thrown, but it could be daunting standing next to some of those tall horses. Among those I took on were Flight, a huge chestnut mare who used to frighten me, and Doctor, an even bigger brown gelding who never bucked but always snorted at me when I caught him, making me think he was untrustworthy. No matter how good I thought I was, there was always a horse or two that could rattle me.

At the end of 1961, at the same dry end as the year before, I wrote to Camboon Station asking for a job. I said in my letter to JTN Bell that I was a keen horseman and had heard about Camboon from Les Cockerill. I received a letter by return mail offering me the full adult wage and asking me when I could start. I left Augustus at the end of the dry season, having been there for almost two years and two full mustering seasons. I had not the slightest notion that I was leaving a life that would change so greatly it would only remain as I chose to remember it.

~

It was after I left Augustus that the relationship between Les Cockerill and Les Briggs went very sour indeed.

Briggs had purchased two unbroken racehorses from Planet Downs. Cockerill and Mrs Briggs formed a very close relationship through their mutual interest in breaking them in and training a winner for the Gregory Cup at the upcoming Easter race meet.

Briggs had been away on a business trip to Cloncurry and on his return decided to drive out to see the ringers at Boundary Camp, a long drive around the river to its main crossing on the road to Gregory and Burketown but only a two-hour ride away if the reason was there. Briggs stopped to open a gate and noticed a fresh set of forward and return horse tracks. When he arrived at Boundary Camp, Briggs asked Alan if he knew anyone who had ridden to the station while he was away. Alan feigned ignorance, but he knew that Cockerill was the night rider. Having seen him saddle and mount his horse after dinner then arrive back at dawn, just in time to join them for breakfast and begin mustering.

Cockerill and Mrs Briggs had developed a relationship beyond the formal and Briggs had his suspicions. The big weekend of the Gregory Cup arrived; the two Augustus horses were to be jockeyed by Cockerill. Trouble was he had plastered himself the night before the race and broken three ribs while negotiating a fence between the pub and his swag. The district nurse enveloped his upper body in strapping to give him some chance of heaping fame on Augustus Downs and Mrs Briggs, in particular. The shining new Augustus silks barely fitted over the strapped Cockerill.

The horse showed no pity; prancing and kicking up, it dislodged Cockerill from the tiny jockey pad. Briggs legged him up again. In pain, and with a hangover and strapped so rigidly that he resembled an Egyptian mummy, Cockerill failed again. When he hit the ground, Briggs sacked him on the spot.

15

CULTURE SHOCK

John Thomas Norton Bell was elegant on foot and horse. Known as 'JTN' or 'Bill' to his friends, he was fifty-one and in the prime of his life when I arrived at Camboon in January 1962. His days on tougher horses were over, but he always looked gathered whenever he rode out to inspect a mob or help us yard up. Secure and confident, he spoke quietly and without hubris or bombast as manager and part-owner of this large and prestigious cattle station owned by a Bell family syndicate that could trace its origins to the ruling side during the first years of the colony.

The Bells of Camboon were direct descendants of Ensign Archibald Bell, who, together with his wife and children, sailed from England to Australia on the *Sophia* in 1806 and joined the 102 Regiment. Soon promoted to lieutenant, he was in command of the Governor's Body Guard of Light Horse when Major Johnston arrested Governor Bligh and was recalled to England to give evidence. Exonerated of any responsibility for that rebellion, he returned to retire to his Belmont Estate at Richmond, north of Sydney.

It was from Belmont that his second son, also named Archibald, surveyed a track over the Blue Mountains to establish a junction with that marked earlier by Blaxland, Wentworth and Lawson. Archibald's track became known as Bell's Line, and what started as a stock route is now Bells Line of Road across the Blue Mountains. For his contribution to the young colony, the young Archibald was awarded a land grant of 1000 acres at Patrick Plains on the Hunter River, which was at that time at the frontier. One of his sons, James Thomas Marsh Bell, went into a partnership with investors that enabled him to venture into larger properties in Queensland.

The 1710-square-kilometre Camboon Station was purchased in 1874 in partnership with a wealthy English investor and named after the Aboriginal word for the rushes that grew around a waterhole on the creek near the present homestead. By 1882 Bell and Hyde had added the 8000-hectare Coochin at Boonah to their holdings, principally as a fattening paddock for Camboon but also as a less stressful place for Bell's wife to live. That was the start of a homestead that remains renowned for its architectural and cultural heritage, with famous guests such as the Duke of Windsor, who left his signature on a wall just before his brief reign as king. Agatha Christie was a guest and put on a concert for the locals.

The table at which we sat for our meals at Camboon, next to the cook's quarters and kitchen, had been made from the huge pine boards that carried on bullock drays the headstone of Anne Reid to her burial site on Camboon Station. She was the wife of the first owner and died on 6 October 1861. That meant this old timber slab hut had been constructed during the violent war between the Aboriginal owners of the upper Dawson River and the white invaders. Around our table we could see two overlapping holes set about a metre apart in the walls that had been designed for a double-barrelled shotgun to cast pellets wide and also allowed a rifle barrel to protrude with enough space around it to set a sight on any attacking Aboriginal people.

A violent war had preceded the purchase of Camboon by the Bells. It began on 27 October 1857 at Hornet Bank, a cattle station near Taroom on the upper Dawson. Eleven people, including the Fraser family owners, were killed by members of the Jiman people, which began a period of reprisals that saw between 150 to 300 Aboriginals of the upper Dawson killed by police and squatter vigilantes. *The Sydney Morning Herald* of 30 November 1857 reported that twenty white settlers were killed by Jiman people in the upper Dawson out of a total of only 180 settlers. Clearly, the Jiman did not see them as settlers but as invaders and proceeded to rid their land of them.

In April 1858, less than a year after the Hornet Bank killings, two Chinese shepherds and two Englishmen yard builders were speared to death on Camboon Station by the Wulli Wulli people whose country it occupied. The Wulli Wulli are neighbours to the Jiman to the north-west and were rumoured to be involved in the Hornet Bank event. Here at Camboon, the scene of the deaths showed that a struggle had occurred and William Walsh, who was the head stockman at Camboon and who discovered the bodies, described the ground as being 'torn up as if by two bulls fighting'.

That was the cliff that divided Black and white, but there were a few people who saw level country. Walsh could speak the language of the Wulli Wulli who gathered at a big bora ground not far from the homestead. That site was still visible in the 1950s and perhaps even in my time, although it was never mentioned. Walsh described big battles between diverse groups of Aboriginal people who gathered near the Camboon homestead and how they would come to the house to have their wounds attended by Mrs Reid. Walsh described the lawn around the homestead as resembling a field hospital.

The war lasted nearly ten years before the horses and rifles of the white invaders overwhelmed the Aboriginal resistance, which was armed only with wooden clubs, spears and bone knives. Warriors became 'station Blacks', with the only reminder of the past conflict buried in journals and, in the case of Camboon, those overlapping holes in a slab hut, their intent still so obviously apparent and yet barely a conversation piece. Now that reminder is gone. The slab hut was blown over by a major storm in 2013 and judged to be beyond repair. The only thing I recall about interaction between white and Black at Camboon was JTN's son Tim telling me that one of his childhood Aboriginal friends warned him he should never use a stick to stir his tea 'because you never know whether someone had wiped their arse with it'.

Over time Camboon had been reduced from its former 1710 square kilometres by subsequent government closer settlement schemes to its present 345 square kilometres. It was still a large property for that part of Queensland and ran 6000 head of horned Hereford breeders. There were no distant cattle camps near crocodiles and pythons.

We ate in the slab hut next to the kitchen and slept in our rooms in the quarters. The horses were trucked out in advance each day to a small paddock surrounding the dip yard we were using. We got up early and had breakfast before bundling into a Land Rover driven by Tim to the yards to catch our horses and begin mustering. There was no stock camp required, except when we stayed in an old cottage at the Woolshed for a few days and ate pre-packed food.

The Woolshed was a former outstation where 6000 Camboon sheep were shorn every year until 1901, when it became too expensive to employ shepherds to protect them from predation by Aboriginal people and dingoes. It turned out to be easier to shoot and poison Aboriginal people than it was to destroy the dingoes, so a move towards cattle, instead of sheep, in these forested parts of Central Queensland was forced on the graziers by the dingo.

Les Cockerill was correct: Camboon had fine horses. It was the people who went with them that were so different from those I had worked with in the Gulf. I had landed back in Barney Joyce territory. Indeed, JTN was married to Barney's sister Minnette. Perhaps I could have gone directly to Camboon had I not worn those shorts and sandshoes only two years earlier, when I arrived at Monto and met Barney. I should, however, thank him because I then would have missed out on the best two years of my early life.

There was a tradition of jackeroos at Camboon living in the big house and dressing for dinner with JTN, Minnie and Tim. They were private school boys whose parents owned properties. We ringers were in-between people—not in and not quite totally out. We did not have our own camp cook and reckoned we got the seconds. Being invited onto the verandah once a month to share a nip of rum with JTN and Tim was as close as we got to the inside of the family. I found I missed the big cattle camps of the north, where the head stockman held his position on ability and the cook did not serve upstairs and downstairs. Like the English TV series, there were things rustling downstairs that were oblivious to them upstairs.

It was in that slab hut, with its quarters located in a room behind the big granite rock chimney, that one quiet Sunday afternoon the station cook invited me to view her family photos. I naïvely agreed, but it slowly dawned on me after being asked to sit on her bed and being shown numerous photos of her in a swimming suit that there was more to this photo opportunity than met the eye.

Not having any experience with women in the real world, let alone with a woman about fifteen years older than me, I politely excused myself, whereupon she said that if I told anyone about her intention then her ten-year-old son would bash me up as soon as he was big enough. She had nothing to worry about anyway: I was an expert, you will recall, in keeping silent on anything to do with emotional responses.

JTN had installed Tim as head stockman. He was friendly, affable and very easy to get along with, but without the commanding good looks of his father or any possibility of acquiring the same reputation as a horseman. John Carsburg, who had been a ringer from the days JTN was in his prime, had no regard for Tim and still deferred to JTN. Sometimes John was a bit kinder and said that Tim had his peculiar walk as a result of polio when he was a child. I said nothing and did not ask. No sunlight reached Tim, who lived in his father's shade.

I would find out many years later that Tim had suffered from a long and difficult birth that left him starved of oxygen to create lasting damage to his gait and balance. That was the reason behind his inability to reach any real competence as a horseman. From that I deduce that John Carsburg was the de facto head stockman all the time Tim was away at Elgin Downs as a jackaroo. There was probably some stirring resentment in John that he would never bring to the surface. I was oblivious to all that sort of thing, being still in the cocoon stage.

Tim was vastly different to the head stockmen I had worked with in the Gulf, where to hold down that position you had to be the best among us. I had to get used to this difference and learn to admire Tim's good-hearted and open nature. I got to respect him for the way he so clearly loved Camboon and worked with abundant good humour and infectious enthusiasm.

There is something else to add here. Years later, when word got out that I was thinking of writing about my ringer days, I received an email from none other than Gary Briggs, Les Briggs's son, and we subsequently talked over the phone.

I warned him there was a story about Les Cockerill that he might not like, but he was unperturbed, saying that he was only a ten-year-old at the time. However, events of a similar nature occurred later and eventually his parents divorced. I talked to Gary about the origin of his father's appointment to Augustus Downs after having worked at Elgin Downs in Central Queensland and asked him whether his father knew a Tim Bell, who had just returned before my arrival at Camboon after being a jackeroo on Elgin Downs. Gary said that his father had mentioned Tim Bell.

Les Cockerill had a long history on Camboon, and I believe it was probably Tim who, when he heard that Briggs got the manager's position at Augustus, recommended he get in touch with Les as a potential head stockman. The entire episode— from Elgin Downs to Augustus Downs, from Cockerill being employed by Briggs and then falling out with him and me then being at Camboon—only covers a very tight and full three years. It would make a circle if there was not a missing piece: none of us knows what happened to Les Cockerill. I have made failed inquiries, but he can happily survive in my head as one of the best horsemen I have ever known.

Another side to Camboon is that there was a sense of stability; four head stockmen in less than three years at Augustus Downs could hardly be called a sign of good management. Here there was a sense of commitment to the station. While I might have been a transient, the other two ringers had been there for years.

John Carsburg had been born on the Woolshed block of Camboon and his mother died at the property when he was ten. His father now managed a Bell property not far away, at Baralaba. John was short and powerfully built, with the chest and broad shoulders of the little big man. He occupied the room next to me in our line of four rooms; the shower and toilet were at one end.

John had animated conversations with himself while asleep that could at times be sufficiently lively to rouse me from my sleep. I was startled awake one 3 am by 'Holy shit, she's going downhill' before John leaped from his bed, straight through a glass pane in a divided window. I found him lying dazed on the verandah and a cut above his eye from jagged broken glass.

The window was divided into four panes, and if you measured the width of John's shoulders and the size of the pane he had gone through, it was an impossible fit. That vehicle going downhill must have been frightening enough to get him through. I woke the Bells and got approval to drive John to Cracow, where there was a small community-based hospital at a gold mine that supported a very basic medical centre. His forehead stitched, we were back at work in the afternoon. He roped himself in bed every night thereafter. This is true.

However, it was not sleepwalking that did him in. Only two years later, after I had gone, John's horse tripped and fell at a benign trot. He came off and landed on his head, suffering permanent brain damage. He lived in a nursing home in Brisbane for another fifteen years, unable to comprehend the world around him.

The other ringer was Alex Saltner, a good-looking Aboriginal man who had been on Camboon for three years and looked set for many more. Alex might have been a 'yella fella' up in the Gulf, but the Act was not in operation down here and he was comfortable in his skin and with everyone around him.

Camboon lay in the heart of the tick belt and every head of cattle required dipping about every six to eight weeks. Even after being dipped, they would soon be covered again in ticks. We started at one end of Camboon branding calves and dipping every head, and when that was done we started all over again. The cattle were forced down a race that led to a large plunge dip with a sudden drop that ensured they were fully drenched before they swam to a gentler set of steps to get out at its other end. They then walked a short distance in the same race to a holding yard.

Any cattle missed at one muster would be covered in ticks when picked up the next time. The number of missed cattle picked up at each muster would have been an accurate quantitative assessment of our mustering ability, but it was not recorded or regarded as significant data.

Polled Herefords were making their mark, yet aficionados of the horned variety were disdainfully saying they lacked bone and scale. Consequently, every calf on Camboon was dehorned with a set of cupped dehorners that would scoop out the horn bud, and the wound was then dusted with a fly repellent.

Calves were weaned at Camboon, but when they were fresh off their mothers they were vulnerable to dingo predation. Some young calves were killed by dingoes and quite a few were bitten; there were obvious wounds such as bite marks, chewed or missing ears or part or all of the tail missing. John was an expert trapper and we learned how to set dingo traps and use strychnine baits.

I had taken on board the view of the dingo being the enemy of the cattle industry and I did not question it. Camboon was inside a dingo fence that stretched all the way from the western border of New South Wales to the base of the Gulf of Carpentaria at the Cloncurry River and back down to Warwick, where it met the Darling Downs–Moreton Rabbit Board fence. Construction of the Queensland fence had started in 1954, and by the time it was completed it was 5680 kilometres long and enclosed sixteen million sheep and 640,000 head of cattle.

That fence is said to have failed, implying that it must have worked for a time. That is a rationalisation: the abundance of dingoes within it, such as at Camboon, was testimony to its folly. The only function it served was to separate two populations of dingoes, which it did not even do very effectively because lack of maintenance meant there was free movement between them. The main reason maintenance was not implemented for the full length of the fence was because the owners of properties along it received an annual subsidy intended for that purpose but used it to meet other more pressing costs, such as servicing bank loans and boarding school fees.

While Camboon remained glued to its horned Herefords, Barney Joyce, less than 100 kilometres away at Eidsvold Station, was breeding Santa Gertrudis cattle from the United States. Being a Brahman and Shorthorn composite breed, Santa Gertrudis carried heat and tick tolerance from its three-eighths

Brahman and good carcass quality from its five-eighths Short-horn. Barney may have thought it was too pointed to give the Bells a Santa Gertrudis bull for Christmas so he gave them a Droughtmaster bull. That bull was never allowed anywhere near their precious Herefords and was relegated to the igno-minious role of servicing the three Jersey station milkers. The milkers had to be dipped along with the Herefords, and when we ran them through the station dip it could not escape our notice that the Droughtmaster bull was either free of ticks or carried so few that he never warranted dipping.

I raised this Droughtmaster advantage with Tim and JTN, emphasising the great saving in cost and labour if Camboon converted its herd to a more tick-tolerant breed of cattle. The answer was 'Camboon has always run Herefords and always will'. That resistance to change was founded on the Bells having been the first people to change from the traditional Shorthorns to Herefords as early as 1895, when their other prize property, Coochin Coochin, was set up as a Hereford stud to provide bulls for Camboon.

Establishing that stud had involved the expensive purchase of an entire stud cattle herd, supplemented by other stud stock from within Australia and imported from England. With that background and selective breeding, Camboon was said to have one of the finest commercial Hereford herds in the country. The Bells had been innovators, but they were not about to do it all over again.

The main cost of dipping was the endless labour that was so easily overlooked because we were so cheap. There was also the cost of the dip and the consequences of handling it so frequently. Tim would open the concentrate Asuntol powder and pour it into a four-gallon drum, add some water and immerse his bare hands in it to break up the lumps before tipping it into the dip to charge it up.

JTN was the horseman and it was his relationship with horses that Les Cockerill had talked about, so I decided to focus on the horses. That turned out to be very good for me, and from that would arise a new opportunity that was different to anything I had done on Augustus. There were good horses on Camboon and, as there were fewer of them, they were worked more consistently, which only made them better.

On one occasion JTN joined us for yarding cattle when I was riding a lovely young mare named Patricia, who did not buck at all when fresh but often did so when she was really tired out. It had been a big day and she was showing signs of going into one of her bucking phases. I was happy to put on a display for the boss and pushed her into a few good bucks. Some weeks later when we were having our monthly nip of rum at the homestead, JTN quietly said to me, 'You did not need to do that.'

That was the second of the two biggest horseriding lessons I learned as a ringer, and they have served me all my life. Les Cockerill taught me that the biggest show you can put on is to make everything look easy. From JTN I learned that you just don't need to prove anything to anyone and that riding horses can be a big ego trap best avoided by employing quiet inner confidence.

Camboon was more accessible to nearby towns and small villages than Augustus had been, and the Bells kindly allowed me to use the Land Rover to get to a rodeo at Eidsvold. I was lucky: I rode time and scored high enough to make the finals. I remember it as if it was yesterday. A handsome Aboriginal rodeo rider congratulated me as I walked into the riders' stand to await my next ride in the final, but that little flutter came to an end when I drew a big bullock that was a Short-horn Brahman cross that threw me just before the time.

My next rodeo was at Dawes, where I came third in the open bullock ride and got a good kick in the head as I dismounted, leaving a nice little lumpy scar that I still have as a reminder. I wrote to Mum and Holm about my exploits and received a stern reply from Holm saying how utterly foolish I was to be doing such dangerous things.

But then luck came my way again: JTN did not hold my foolish display against me and asked me to become the full-time racehorse trainer for the two Camboon racehorses. It was late winter (there were quite distinct seasons here) and the spring racing season was looming. Among them was the Camboon Cup, to be run at the nearby racetrack. Becoming the racehorse trainer was a truly wonderful experience and I thank the Bells for it. This career change rescued me from dipping and introduced me to trackwork in a jockey pad and getting to know two horses very well.

Marbuk had been broken in at Camboon and, having been used for cattle work by Tim, was responsive and easy to handle. Jourita was a racehorse purchased in Brisbane and racing was all he knew; an hour on him every morning left me with aching arms holding him at a steady trot, even at a time when I was strong enough. My routine was to get up well before dawn and do an hour of roadwork on each horse. Once or twice I took them to the track and JTN gave me instructions on the pace and furlong distance for each horse.

After breakfast I cleaned out the stables, groomed the horses and checked the soundness of the heavier shoes the racecourse farrier had put on them after the light racing plates were removed. In the afternoon I took them on long and relaxed walks. I did odd jobs around the station, but the horses were my primary responsibility.

Unlike at Augustus, it was possible to meet real live women at Camboon. I silently lusted after two lovely young women who worked as domestics. One was of Aboriginal and Chinese descent, and the racial mix produced a walking, talking delight. I didn't have the courage to mention my thoughts, far less act on them. They showed no interest in me and I stayed in my comfort zone of revealing nothing about what I would really like to do with either of them.

Sue appeared suddenly. She was supposed to be something like a jillaroo; she lived with the Bells, although we weren't sure of her role or whether she was a paid member of staff. We concluded her mission was to land a grazier husband, with Tim the frontrunner. We were on the mark, because a mating ritual danced in the horse yard every morning. One of us had to saddle Nimrod, one of JTN's quiet horses, then Sue would arrive in form-fitting moleskins, her cheeks powdered and a beacon of red lips below blue eye shadow. She was far outside my experience and evoked curiosity without arousal. She stayed for a month or so then left; Tim remained single.

I did not fully appreciate the fact that the hotels at Theodore were near enough for a Saturday night drink, which broke up the work routine and camaraderie. Many of my weekends were spent alone but I did sometimes accompany John and Alex to the pub, and a barmaid asked John to arrange a date with me. I took it up and we went to the movies at Theodore. She was nice and easy to get along with, but I made no move to arrange another meeting. I look back on it and wonder why. I was needy enough.

The Camboon Cup was a major social event and many hundreds of people travelled long distances to attend it. The Bells hosted many friends and relatives. Marbuk won the cup, and the Bells were thrilled and proud and thanked me profusely for my training effort. I continued training Marbuk and Jourita and they were taken to race meetings further afield.

Barney Joyce would have been a guest, but I did not seek him out to attempt any conversation or recollection of our earlier meeting in Eidsvold; such was the class difference between ringer and owner. That came up again at the race-day ball held at the Camboon community hall. I was asked to dance by the beautiful blonde daughter of a prominent grazing family but I shyly declined. I had already built my own strong barrier between management and staff. I was just a ringer, and she was in another cultural system. My insecurity used race, occupation, age and concept of class to keep at bay the few women I met.

I received an unexpected letter from Mum to say she was coming up to discuss what would be my last opportunity to go to Hawkesbury Agricultural College. If I declined this time my name would be removed from the enrolment list. I still had no real enthusiasm for doing this; having found my voice as a ringer, I did not want to fail in a different choir. I asked the Bells for permission for Mum to spend the night in one of the spare rooms in the ringers' quarters. She drove all the way from Sydney in a second-hand Skoda, accompanied by my young brother Chris and one of his friends.

I had considered Augustus Downs completely out of range for Mum, with the lack of accommodation as the barrier, whereas the trip from Sydney to Camboon was possible even though it was a major undertaking. Mum drove into Camboon with Chris poking his air rifle out of one window and his friend poking his air rifle out of the opposite window. They were happy and excited and I was deeply embarrassed, hoping that no one had seen them arrive. There was no way to get inside the Bell tent with a family like that.

Mum and I sat on the bank of the creek near the homestead. I looked at her and noticed grey flecks in her hair. I was eighteen and she was fifty-one, and it was the instant I realised that even my mother could age. I felt deeply sad that I had missed every opportunity to relate to her on any other level but the formal.

She counselled me at the right time. Without our conversation that day I would have seen the year out at Camboon and then gone back north the following year. In my young and adventurous head there was also a strong desire to go to Argentina and be a gaucho, but with no definite plan and wanting to please her, since she had gone to so much effort, I agreed to go to Hawkesbury.

That was the beginning of a return to the education I had only four years previously solemnly vowed never to partici-pate in again.

EPILOGUE

I sometimes joke that my education began a long downhill slope. Not very funny, although there is an element of truth to it. Probably this is my way of protecting those three years as a ringer, because I don't want them lost as a rite of passage to somewhere else. Everything led to those years, which contained and then shaped everything that followed— just as they had shaped me. Then it started all over again at Hawkesbury, and this is how it went from there.

On arrival at the college on a Sunday afternoon, ready for a shaky start, I was greeted by third-year students in weird clothes with attitude. I thought their demands were a humorous affair and responded in language that had previously worked well for me. They called themselves 'sirs' and we were Motts, each of us named from a vocabulary honed by years of tradition. For my resistance, before I learned that being obscure would make the process easier, I became Mott Hymen. 'And why are you called Mott Hymen, Mott?' to which there was a standard reply that each of us was obliged to reply. In my case it was 'Because I am going to be broken, sir'. The only thing we saw of officialdom during Motting Week was Roger Roberts, the farm machinery teacher, who was a Hawkesbury Agricultural College graduate. Talk about the fox being in charge of the hen house.

I got through all of that—supposedly with a vibrant new college spirit, the excuse for the Motting. This time I was not disappointed by image. Hawkesbury Agricultural College had an Ivy League graciousness that fitted its reputation. The brick and tile dormitories and lecture rooms were surrounded by neatly laid out paddocks separating the variety of agricultural enterprises, each with their own operational headquarters and animal complexes. Dairy, beef cattle, sheep, poultry, piggery, apiary and orchard sections all laid out in an orderly fashion. First-year students spent two days a week on farm duty and we were rostered on all the different sections of the college to gain practical experience—and earn our keep, I suspect. There were some tractors that full-time farmhands used, and we got horse and cart.

I learned how to study parrot fashion. Not hard to do at Hawkesbury, where analysis and wrestling with ideas was not expected and regarded as downright dangerous. I performed reasonably well in the exams. Nothing outstanding, but with a bit of effort I regularly came between seventeenth and twentieth in a year of about seventy students. One term exam crash to near the bottom of the class was a reminder that fun was not an examinable subject. At the end of the year I managed to win a Department of Agriculture cadetship, which meant I received a weekly stipend and had all my fees paid for the next two years.

Some of my fellow students already had steady girl-friends. Others had gone to co-ed schools and knew how to interact with women, and they arranged blind dates for me. Another had a sister who held some attraction. Once a month the Richmond RSL had a dance for teenagers and I met local girls. The college had a gracious ballroom for our end-of-term dance and I wanted to be a part of that, so at the ripe old age of nineteen I stepped out of a life among male ringers into the much more complex world of men and women.

Snake handling was added to my list of livestock subjects by fellow student Jack Rhodes. Jack was a walking, talking snake charmer who could get red-bellied black snakes loosely hanging over him and living freely in his bedroom. I gravitated to Jack, anxious to add his skill set to mine.

Jack and I caught many snakes and kept some of the larger specimens alive in our rooms. We jammed a towel into the gap beneath the door to ensure they didn't injure themselves in trying to escape. They would curl up on our beds in the warmth of the day and find a way under the blankets or pillows when requiring cover.

We were spoilt brats at Hawkesbury. Our beds were made each day; our rooms were swept out and our windows cleaned; our sheets and towels were changed weekly. This was all done by stewards who were recent arrivals from countries where snakes were small and fear was big. Jack and I asked them not to do our rooms while snakes were in residence, but when the steward who serviced our wing was off sick, his replacement, undeterred by the towel jammed under the door, went in to make my bed. He raised the crumpled blanket to find three large red-bellied black snakes curled up under it, then screamed and ran in fright. The stewards downed brooms and went on strike, refusing to return to work until all snakes were removed.

John Kienzle, a second-year student, came from a large rubber plantation in Kokoda in Papua New Guinea. I had little contact with John because the hierarchy of seniority limited interaction between the years, but I had heard that a couple of his friends at college had gone to work on the Kienzle family plantation during the long summer vacation. I approached John and asked if he knew of plantation owners who might provide me a similar opportunity. He said he would think about it and let me know.

A month later John said I could go to work on their property provided I broke in three horses for them. They paid my entire return airfare to Kokoda and I joined them in their beautiful home on the banks of the Mamba River. Here, as distinct from those Camboon days, I sat at the table with Bert Kienzle at its head and with Mrs Kienzle at the other end.

It was impossible to avoid the esteemed reputation held by Bert Kienzle and his role in organising the native porters, or Fuzzy Wuzzy Angels, carrying supplies across the Kokoda Track to repel the Japanese invasion during the Second World War. Bert knew the people, their language and the terrain, and every book written on the Kokoda Track refers to the work of Bert Kienzle.

Bert was a big strong man who now limped due to an arthritic hip that gave him constant pain he never mentioned. He was of German and Samoan descent, the first of these heritages meant he was interned in Australia at Bourke and Molonglo during the First World War. While Bert was interned my father was fighting on the German side, but their roles were reversed during the Second World War, with my father interned and Bert fighting for Australia. Following his work as a goldminer, Bert established Mamba Estates at Kokoda. His loyalty was never questioned when Japan invaded New Guinea on its thwarted march to Australia.

Not long after John's younger brother Soccer and I had undertaken a long hike up the Kokoda Track as far as Isurava to arrange a new supply of fresh vegetables from various villages along the track, Bert called me into his office for a chat about my future. He said he wanted to extend the cattle operation at Kokoda to a new property at Popondetta, the capital of Oro Provence about 80 kilometres from Kokoda. He offered to purchase the entire property, build the infrastructure, stock it with cattle and give me half-ownership of the entire operation from day one.

I was overwhelmed by such generosity and that he could see something in the twenty-year-old me. John told me later that Bert had liked my work ethic and attitude and had said to John that it arose from my German background. That was a definite first! I was not aware it was a factor at the time, but Holm had had some success in drumming an organised way of working into my young head, consolidated by my years as a ringer.

I thanked Bert but said that since I was now bonded to the Department of Agriculture, I wanted to see that out and take a position with them when I graduated. The bond itself was not a major impediment as it could be paid out, however, Bert understood and simply said that the offer remained open if I changed my mind. At the end of my cadetship I planned on becoming a livestock officer for beef cattle, horses and goats, that is, an extension officer working with farmers to help them increase production and profitability.

Hawkesbury Agricultural College was incredibly kind to me right to the end. In my third and final year I was selected by the head of the Arab stud to be his groom at the Royal Easter Show. The monosyllabic George Thomson was the head groom and my boss at the showground. It was a fantastic experience working with the two stallions, Babylon and Theseus, along with two mares. Next to the stables was a tent music show featuring three kids who called themselves the Bee Gees.

There were no vacancies in the beef cattle section when I graduated, so I was assigned as a livestock officer for poultry at the Department of Agriculture's Grantham Poultry Research Station at Seven Hills. Being exposed to thousands of chooks every day, I learned some of the basics of managing large numbers of them. I could spot sick chooks and do a basic post-mortem to find common problems.

Then came an opportunity to be part of the crew on a beautiful big yacht in a race from Sydney to Noumea. With a lot of wrangling, and my rapid-response promise that I would do a survey of the poultry industry in New Caledonia, I was granted six weeks' leave without pay. We moored at the Noumea Yacht Club in that beautiful French colonial town, unchallenged by the tourist boom to come. That none of us could speak French did not impede our enjoyment.

Despite the distractions, I still needed to meet my obligation to write a report on the poultry industry. I needed to meet someone in the New Caledonian equivalent of a Department of Agriculture, then it was finding someone who had anything to do with poultry. I finally met a man who worked for such a government entity and whose responsibilities involved poultry. Despite his English being limited and my conversational French being zero, we made sufficient communication and ended up driving out to a large egg and poultry meat operation just outside Noumea. It sat beside a tranquil lagoon inlet from the sea, a location more appropriate for a luxury tourist resort than for the sprawling sheds of a large industrial poultry farm.

I was introduced to a staff member and the three of us commenced the inspection. As we passed along the rows of hens in their egg-laying cages, I noticed some of them were not thriving and had symptoms of disease. Being something of a poultry expert, I suspected they were suffering from coccidiosis, a parasitic disease of the intestines caused by coccidian protozoa, which thrives in humid conditions; that the site was beside a tropical sea made it an immediate suspect. Some individual fowls can develop immunity but that only helps to pass it on. The most satisfactory treatment is medication delivered in the watering system.

I had been guided in performing post-mortems that show if this disease is present. In sign language with a finger across my throat, I was given five sick hens to depart this paradise by the sea and enter chook heaven. I was very confident in confirming my initial diagnosis of coccidiosis and could indicate it to those present. I then recommended the appropriate medication that could easily be delivered to every bird through the watering system.

When our tour finished, my French agricultural officer and I returned to the car. I sat in the passenger seat while he spent some time saying goodbye to the manager. He returned and explained in broken English that the person who had showed us around was actually the owner of the poultry farm and a prominent businessman in Noumea. He said the owner had asked him to offer me the position of manager of the entire operation. I need not worry about any minor details such as immigration or barriers to residency, because all that would be dealt with. Moreover, I would be given a house by the lagoon to live in and a vehicle for business and personal use on top of a generous wage.

My answer was the same as to Bert Keinzle: I had my heart set on being a beef cattle officer and all I had to do when I got back was wait for a vacancy. Finally, a vacancy did arise and I was sent to spend time in training with Jim Beck, the beef cattle officer at Lismore. I travelled the district with him for six months. Many years later he wrote about me in a departmental journal:

On the day in question our programme was to look at the weaners and talk about supplementary feeding. Mrs Hodgson was to check the calving cows on the western side of the property while Ray and I went to look at the weaners. Rolly went with Mrs Hodgson. After a couple of hours riding, moving cattle and discussing the options with fodder and grass available, Ray and I returned to the homestead expecting the others to be home but there was no sign of them. We put our horses in the yard and were heading over to the house when we saw the pair coming up the road. Rolly was out in front holding a bag at arm's length wearing a big smile. Apparently he had spotted a big goanna going up a tree and by standing on the saddle was able to grab it by the tail.

After lunch we set off back to Lismore. The stench of that goanna in the station wagon on a hot day was almost unbearable but no amount of talking would get Rolly to give up his new found pet. He took it home to his flat in Ballina and left it in the laundry overnight. He made a collar for it, put it on a dog chain and pegged it out on the front lawn but it would not eat so he eventually set if free.

I am not sure about the standing in the saddle part. Maybe I stood up in the stirrups because standing in the saddle to catch a big goanna on a strange horse would be tough, but that is the way he told it. Jim died of Parkinson's disease, and his wife, Lola, married his brother not long after he came out for the funeral. I stayed in contact with Lola until her very old age.

From Lismore I was sent back to the Hawkesbury Agricultural College's beef cattle section as a junior officer, which is basically a tutor. Ben Andrews, who had been my lecturer as a student, now became my great mentor and a lifelong friend. It was his recommendation that I was posted to my first district, at Tumut.

There was a drought burning the eastern Riverina hills when I arrived in Tumut in the winter of 1968. Keen to advance my career in the Agriculture Department, I wrote an article on the early weaning of calves and feeding them well for growth and production and putting the cows on a maintenance ration to save money during dry times. I sent the draft up to Bill Murphy, a veterinary graduate who was head of the beef cattle section, to approve it for publication as one of the department's advisory leaflets.

Murphy replied after about a fortnight with an utterly stinging and brutally frank criticism of my writing. My draft had a red pen through it with a 'Rubbish' spiced with a 'What do you mean?' His final comment was 'Go and do some reading yourself before you try and write anything. The Bible would be a good start.' Why the Bible, or was I so hopeless at writing that the Bible was all Murphy could come up with? There was nothing acknowledging my initiative; nothing about a good try and here are some suggestions. The Bible remains unread by me to the present day.

There was a strong network of fellow beef cattle officers in other regions who would have been pleased to help me get my early weaning publication into print. My mentor, Ben Andrews, would have guided me past that setback if I had confided in him, but my emotional secrecy kept my angst in its familiar cave.

A vacancy arose as assistant education officer with the newly created New South Wales National Parks and Wildlife

Service (NPWS). Anne, the beautiful and gifted art teacher at Tumut High School, said that if I got the position she would apply for a transfer to Sydney. I won the job and her at the same time, and we were married the following year, in May 1969. The big surprise to me when I arrived at my new job was that I was the assistant education officer with no one to assist. Allan Fox, the previous education officer, had transferred to another position.

With Bill Murphy's assessment fresh in mind, I searched unsuccessfully for a writing course I could enrol in. There was nothing available that I could attend or participate in. But then I found a way to avoid a confrontation with the pen by giving slide show talks to whoever would listen. Day or night, week or weekend, in cold halls or sunny afternoon Scouts or Girl Guides camps, I would be there. Rotary, Apex and Lions clubs, Country Women's Association conferences, amateur bird-watching groups, bushwalking clubs, Masons—you name it.

I set up a screen on its tripod stand, and with a two-slot slide projector gave my talks on national parks and wildlife conservation. Sometimes I humped along an old film projector that I threaded with scratched film. Hard to believe now, with so much material available and so easily presented in Power-Point, that in 1969 I would show the Walt Disney film *The Living Desert*, which had been filmed in the United States, and use it to explain how its ecological principles could be applied to Australia. The only Australian films—and they were films on reels—were *Brolga* by Harold Pollard and *The Mallee Fowl* by Harry Frith. They were a long way from Sundance, Cannes and the Oscars, but people liked them, and I liked that.

Lacking a university degree, I had reached the end of the road and the position of education officer was advertised. It was made abundantly clear to me that I should not waste any time applying, because an appropriate university degree was essential. There had been no discrimination between diploma holders and university graduates in the Department of Agriculture, and selection for senior positions came from both streams. Moreover, many of the senior officers in that department were graduates of Hawkesbury Agricultural College, so there was a well-established old boys' network right to the top. Being regarded by the NPWS as unqualified for the position that I thought I was filling so well was downright painful, but I really liked my job and had no intention of resigning.

I made an appointment with the head of the department, Don McMichael. He knew me well enough, because the NPWS was still small enough for him to take a personal interest in it. I confided to him that I was facing a degree barrier, and he said very simply and so directly that I could not escape my response: 'Roland, you come up with a plan and I will support you all the way.' That support amounted to me going to back to Hawkesbury on full pay to complete the first postgraduate Certificate in Rural Extension. The head of the course was Grahame Bird, who was at the forefront of self-directed adult learning. I thrived in that environment, and Grahame exhumed an ambition for a more meaningful education that must have been buried deep within me.

The early 1970s was the age of the T group: sensitivity training workshops led by a facilitator. These were beneficial for me and led me to seek further counselling to shed some of the outsider feelings that still haunted me.

The postgraduate diploma gave me graduate status in the NPWS at last, but something had now been awoken and I enrolled as an external student at the University of New England. I loved every minute of the five years it took, over nights and weekends, to graduate. That was followed by other postgraduate studies that turned around my young disdain for education.

In 1972 the newly elected Whitlam government decided to create the Commonwealth Department of Environment and Conservation, with grand plans to create a network of national parks across Australia. Don McMichael was recruited as its head. Not long afterwards I resigned from the NPWS to take up a position in the new department. My new boss was Dr Robert Boden, who became another mentor and, like Don, would transition into a dear friend. By this time I had done some writing, and Robert now patiently helped me achieve accuracy and economy of words in writing cabinet submissions and reports.

Anne and I had owned a home on the edge of a large bushland reserve at Cheltenham in northern Sydney. That was hard to give up, so instead of buying a house in Canberra we purchased 'Hilltop' farm at Candelo in the Bega Valley and went there from our rented flat every weekend. Anne had transferred from being art teacher at Cheltenham High to Queanbeyan High.

Sir John Kerr saved me from a life behind a desk. I was building some cattle yards at Hilltop the day Malcolm

Fraser won the election following the Whitlam dismissal, and I wanted to take the Monday as leave to get the job finished. I was urged to return to Canberra immediately to put my name forward for a suitable position in the department subject to major change. I simply said: 'Leave me out of it and I will resign gracefully as soon as possible.' Anne did the same, and we took up full-time residence on the farm. I picked up some consultancy work and broke in horses for a living. Anne taught part-time at the local TAFE. We still had a debt and had to buy cattle for our farm.

Mum had left two brothers behind in Germany and they eventually contacted her. As the only Breckwoldt in Australia, she would not have been hard to find. With her parents now dead, she inherited her rightful share of the family farm in Schleswig-Holstein. With this she built a small cottage at Wentworth Falls, where she started spending more time.

Holm suffered a stroke and became bedridden and was cared for by Mum. I was a very deficient son, heavily involved in self and work and new marriage. It got too hard for Mum and Holm entered a nursing home for his final months. He was always half sitting up in his bed and half lying down and wearing a bib. Unrecognisable as the man with whom I had worked so hard in the garden. Yet, he could still offer advice. He said: 'Son, you will be surprised how fast your life goes.' Correct on that one.

His life ended on 12 December 1973 at the age of eighty-one and only two years after he retired. He was cremated at the Northern Suburbs crematorium; only his immediate family and some of Anne's family attended. No tears were shed. No friend or even an acquaintance in sight. Funeral attended; obligation fulfilled. It would take another four decades for a soft thought to emerge within me from that deep, distant abyss.

Mum sold the house at North Rocks to the Catholic Church, which promptly flattened the house and garden Holm and I had toiled over. The only remnant is a big stone barbecue that he built thinking we would all be sitting around it with him, but that never happened. Mum moved to her little house in Wentworth Falls and North Rocks changed from bush to urban.

A couple of years after Anne and I bought Hilltop we purchased another 162-hectare farm next door. Mum moved there and helped care for our son, Dan, born, to our great joy, in February 1978. Along came 1983, which was a very big year. It began with the publication of my book *Wildlife in the Home Paddock*, which had been in the making for over three years of effort circumscribed by trepidation. Maybe my self-doubt pushed me along, because it became a great success. The first edition sold out in less than three months and it went on to another two editions.

In May my good friend George Wilson, an avid pilot, rang me to say he wanted to fly his six-seater Cessna to Darwin for a wildlife conference and asked if Anne, Dan (now four years old) and I would like to join him, Lyn and their own four-year-old son, Edward, on the flight north. In planning the flight I suggested a stop at Augustus Downs. Once the decision had been made I contacted Augustus, still communicating by telegram through the Royal Flying Doctor Service channel: 'Ringer 1960–1962 dearly like to visit. Will be in light plane. OK to refuel? Will be independent.' The reply came next day: 'OK to refuel. Be independent.'

This time we landed on the airstrip right next to the station. Parked at the end of it was the station's Cessna, and nearby was a semitrailer fitted for livestock. The relentless advance of technology was obvious. The manager's house was air-conditioned and in the office below it hung New South Wales NPWS wildlife posters, the same ones that had been painted by Margaret Senior during my time there.

The 'be independent' faded, and Phillip and Adele Hughes made us more than welcome. They assigned us a Toyota to use, and we drove out to camp with swags and a tent that Anne and Dan slept in. I insisted on rolling out the same swag I had used in my ringer days, so I could look at the stars. Mosquitoes got me more than I remembered.

Augustus had changed. It was now owned by Stanbroke Pastoral Company and had gradually but surely been turned into the showplace it is today. By that 1983 visit the Short-horn cattle had been totally replaced by 15,000 Brahman breeders. The fencing required for the brucellosis eradication scheme meant that cows were being weaned of their calves. That alone doubled the branding rate from my time.

There was a big steel cattle yard at Dinner Camp Bore. Bronco yards were a thing of the past. The Top End, including my beloved Disraeli, was entirely fenced off during the brucellosis eradication scheme and remained unused. It would eventually be involved in a land swap with Lorraine-Tallawanta.

No longer was a lot of time taken to ride out from the

camps. Early in the morning a truck took the horses out to a predetermined spot so the ringers could muster in. Now only one horse was required for the day. The Cessna flew overhead and dropped notes wrapped in pebbles and caught in hats to locate mobs and any cattle missed.

A dramatic change was the abundance of the Agile wallaby (*Macropus agilis*). They had been a rare sight in my time, only twenty years earlier. I would occasionally see one hopping madly out of sight along the steep banks of the Leichhardt River; now they were in plague proportions. The explanation for this lay in the Cessna and mechanisation in the form of more and faster vehicles on more frequently graded station roads. This meant 1080 (sodium fluoroacetate), which had been around since the 1950s, could be baited with meat right on hand and spread with ease. With the dingo predator gone, the Agile wallabies partied.

I sat around with a few of the ringers and showed them my photo album. They clearly enjoyed looking at them. There were no Aboriginal ringers in a separate camp now and none among them, although a couple appear in recent photos of Augustus Downs available on a Kent Saddlery website and they are a full part of the team with equality.

The big semitrailer carried cattle and the Augustus Downs polocrosse team to games at places as far away as Julia Creek. Not even in our wildest foresight, and certainly not in Rabbit's prophecies of doom, could any of us have imagined Augustus Downs supporting its own polocrosse team. These were not weekly events, but they were frequent enough for them all to wear branded shirts.

I asked Phillip whether this was a team-building exercise, and he said that the original intention was as a social outlet and to build a quality team. A noticeable result was a greater commitment to their work in a more harmonious camp. No longer are the dry camps imposed by Reg Nissen acceptable and alcohol is allowed in the wet camps of today. Moreover, there is a heady mix of male and female ringers with trouble brewing, if you will pardon the pun, if there is not appropriate training. These days a head stockman will have attended many training sessions and may have done a Myers-Briggs or two to hone their management skills.

Back at the station I got to know Phillip. He had been born on Nockatunga Station in the far south-west of Queensland and became a head stockman at the age of seventeen. He is a gifted horseman and tells great stories, so it was inevitable we would click and form a lifelong and very dear friendship. We visit them; they visit us.

After managing Bulloo Downs, Phillip resigned from Stanbroke to take over his family property, Banchory Station, at Clermont, about 100 kilometres north-west of Emerald. I visited them and in 2018 acted as his caretaker manager while he and Adele took leave. They only recently sold Banchory and now operate a large paddock-to-plate operation at Dulacca. Distance is an issue, but we are on the phone to each other every other week. There is no problem in talking about or reliving the ringer days in the Gulf, and our conversations keep me attached to that Queensland big country.

~

Mum did have some happy times, when her life became less turbulent with age. She lived in a big brick Federation homestead overlooking the gentle hills of the Bega Valley, a garden around her and a new grandson nearby. She was sixty-eight when she arrived, but her ability to drive and her independence disappeared at seventy when she crashed her car twice in quick succession on the quiet road leading to her house, the second one causing her car's destruction. The crash of her short-term memory was underway and I wish, so very much, I had picked that up much earlier.

She wanted so badly to stay in her own home, and through her fog I became her brother. We eventually set up an emergency monitor for her, but she would see the little indicator light at night and turn it off to save electricity. Anne and I purchased her food and the occasional bottle of sherry. She could no longer turn the TV on and off or select any channels. The bottle of sherry would get consumed in one night and, no longer remembering to eat or drink, she would retreat to her bed and stay there without food and water.

Anne and I followed the ambulance to the Bega nursing home, wracked by our personal grief at Mum making this final journey out of the home she loved, where all her Chinese antiques and the Quan Yin statue cast their aura over the lounge room. All this was replaced by a bed and a cupboard in a shared room.

Mum thought the garden around the nursing home was hers, and in the absence of secateurs she took to improving the landscaping by breaking off branches that offended her. She got aggressive when anyone else met their visitors in the room set aside for new arrivals. After that we noticed the big change as she sat silently among the old, not interacting, but her face would light up as I, her dear brother, and Anne entered the room. She always wanted us to stay and have dinner with her. I made excuses.

I was now often travelling to distant and remote Aboriginal lands as a consultant. I made the trip to Alice Springs on thirty-three occasions, to travel out from there to remote Aboriginal communities. It was my turn to contribute to Aboriginal people with cattle management and feral animal harvesting and control. They now told me what to do, and I enjoyed where it led.

Good fortune had me at home when the phone rang at 11.30 pm to hear that Mum had been transferred to Bega Hospital with a suspected perforated bowel. I asked the prognosis and the nurse said it was not good and I should wait until the morning, when the doctor would make an assessment.

The last words Mum spoke, as her face lit up for the last time, were, 'It is lovely to see you.' It did not matter in the slightest that I was not her brother; those words defined her life. She was wheeled away and came back sedated beyond communication. There were many at her funeral. I felt it and wanted them there. Some said I made a moving eulogy.

There was a thud on the carpeted floor of her study as we cleaned her house: it was a sealed plastic container with a typed label stating it contained the ashes of Alfred Holm Breckwoldt. It had been with Mum all those years since his death and none of us knew it, but had been found just in time for Holm's ashes and Mum's to lie together under a granite slab at the tiny Tantawangalo cemetery, only a kilometre from where she lived. Presumably there are no arguments, as now there is no distance between them.

The German that I hated so much remains the only living link I have with Holm and Mum. Any poor German tourist within earshot is a victim of my language practice. They say that I speak Hochdeutsch, and many ask what part of Germany I come from. I tell myself that 'Sometime I will get there'.

Our son, Dan, did get there and spent six months during a high school gap year with my cousin, who was head of the water police at Kiel. Dan arrived back totally obsessed with living in Europe. He had learned that access to a German passport and citizenship was patrilineal. Since I had been born a British citizen and was now Australian, it turned out to be a dead end. Dan, being quick of mind, said, 'You get your passport, so then I can get mine.'

It occurred to me that since Holm was interned there must be some record of his German passport or other official record to the same effect. I rang the Department of Defence and was directed to a helpful person; he said they didn't hold that material but I should try the Central Army Records Office in Melbourne. I called them and another kind person said: 'Sorry, mate, we only hold records of Australian soldiers. Why don't you try the [National] Archives?' By the way, this was long before the internet.

The person who answered the phone at the archives took my details and said he would contact me if anything was found.

About a fortnight later he rang with: 'You will indeed be interested in what we hold about your father. Send us a cheque for $80 and we will copy it and put it in the post.' In that treasure trove of family history was a photocopy of Holm's passport and his many submissions to obtain Australian citizenship.

With confirmation that Holm and Mum were Germans when I was born, Dan got his German passport in 1995 with ease and used it to work in London when the UK was still in the EU. I saw no need for a German passport until my grandson, Max, was born in Vancouver in December 2015. A sense of continuity prompted me to breathe life back into the German kid I had once been.

The German Embassy in Canberra did not welcome me at all in 2016, when illegal immigration, document theft and the use of multiple identities had intervened since Dan's application had sailed through. The German Embassy made me jump through one hoop after the other and wanted to divert me through a long and cumbersome German citizenship application. I knew how far that would get me.

They demanded nothing short of the original of Holm's German passport and the National Archives would not release it. Eventually the embassy accepted a National Archives certified copy and granted my German passport. I held that passport when it arrived and suddenly felt whole. All those childhood attempts to deny my origins disappeared.

'Breckwoldt' sounds good to me now. Johannes I can live with, noting that it is not as uncommon a name in Australia as it once was. My German passport rests in a drawer in the lamp stand beside my bed, a curiosity to show friends.

I toy with using it one day. I have travelled a lot but never to Germany, perhaps because I have already experienced it.

Now I live in the Southern Highlands and spend my time in our big garden, riding my three horses and working on local farms to keep me engaged in the broader community. I also teach some horseriding, which helps me complete the circle. Before that I did ten years in the corporate world as a consultant, which took me all over Australia on big evaluations of Commonwealth government–funded programs managed by the states and territories.

Many projects, such as an evaluation of the Great Artesian Basin Sustainability Initiative, involved assessment of case studies on large cattle and sheep stations across Australia. Another consultancy project on changes in natural resource management had me headed for interviews in Emerald, Queensland. I made sure they were on a Friday so I could visit over the weekend with Phillip and Adele Hughes at Banchory Station at Clermont. When I arrived there I met Bill Hughes, Phillip's father, who had been instrumental in adding Augustus Downs to the Stanbroke Pastoral Company holdings all those years ago. He was now over eighty and ramrod straight; he planned to join us for a muster to get cattle ready for sale.

I woke at dawn for a steak breakfast before we departed in a truck with our horses on board to a distant paddock. Horses unloaded, saddled and ready, Phillip drew a mud map plan to muster cattle and take them to a central meeting point. The others rode off in different directions. I joined Phillip and rode out with him for the day. Two Gulf riders together. Me, a ringer again.

ACKNOWLEDGEMENTS

My adorable sister, Angela, spent four years of her early childhood in the internment camp and committed her memories to paper for me. My thanks to her while deeply regretting her experience. I thank my dear son, Dan. If not for his determination to get a German passport, a treasure trove of family history would have remained among the skeletons. The same dearest thanks to Anne for her support and her eclectic reading that reflects light my way.

Thanks to the anonymous people in the Department of Defence and the Australian Archives in Canberra, and Central Army Records in Melbourne, who answered my phone calls and were so abundantly helpful in exposing family skeletons to the light making sense of a past I can call upon.

In late 2015 I met Hugh Mackay at a local function, and I could not help but mention my project. He recommended an editor, Deonie Fiford. Anxious for some feedback, I sent her a letter with some very rough chapters. She wrote to me in February 2016 saying that she was too busy to take on another client but attached to her letter was a generous six-page review of all the chapters. She suggested that I could self-publish or, if I worked hard on it, I might find a publisher. I thank Deonie for her kind and thoughtful review. Tim Flannery read some of my attempts to put Deonie's comments into practice and surprised me by asking for more about those ringer days. Later, Irina Dunn sagely advised me to take my time until I could bear reading it aloud to myself. Not sure I got there Irina, but you helped me find a voice.

Thanks to my dear friends Phillip and Adele Hughes who reviewed what I wrote about those days in the Gulf and were so complimentary about it. Other good friends, David and Mary Marsh, read the draft manuscript and their unstinting encouragement spurred me into shaping it for an unknown reader who might hopefully feel the same.

Alan Candlish and Ralph Tate refresh the mental maps of our ringer days. Luckily, we are still on the right side of the soil and can have a long-distance yarn about things long past. Alan also drew the lines of the map of Augustus. Thanks to the many people I rang with so many questions, among them Bob Carsburg, Helen Peut, Jeff Nissen, Alec Saltner, Ian Varidel, Sue Bell, Tim and Jane Bell, John Keinzle, Ian de Satge and John Blay. Thanks also to Gary Briggs who contacted me while writing his memoir and shared his father's background.

Having been the publisher of my first book, *Wildlife in the Home Paddock*, when CEO of Angus & Robertson where he and editor Mary Coleman nursed it into print, I was so fortunate to find Richard Walsh again, now in the Allen & Unwin paddock. When flicking through the Saturday *Australian* I happened to read an interview with Bryan Brown about his book in which he paid tribute to Richard. An instant phone call to Allen & Unwin had me emailing Richard via their nuisance screen. Within the hour came a welcome response from Richard offering to read a couple of chapters. He read them and asked for the rest that he pruned and edited with a deft and graceful hand. Rebecca Kaiser and her team at Allen & Unwin then put their microscope to it. More editing. Questions. Clarifications. Formatting. Photos. Artwork. All so collaboratively. So smoothly. Such an absolute pleasure working with them. I sincerely hope my gratitude to Richard and Rebecca and all their colleagues shows within the pages.

GLOSSARY

bronco horse: a larger, heavier stockhorse selected for the role of pulling calves up to the bronco ramp.

bronco ramp: a sloping rail on posts that leads to a gap of about 10 centimetres between another post and level rail. The rider lassoes a calf and drags it behind the sloping rail until the rope falls between the slot, then it is pulled up for the ground crew to put leg ropes on and pull it by the tail until in is on the ground with the leg ropes attached to pegs on the ramp. That describes the permanent ramps at Augustus, but there are many temporary adaptations.

bronco yard: a yard with posts usually strung with wire or old cable in which cattle are placed so the cleanskin calves can be lassoed and pulled up to the bronco ramp to be earmarked, inoculated and branded, and the males castrated.

bull: if branded, then a male deliberately kept for breeding.

bullock: a castrated male three years of age or older; the product taken by the drover to the railhead at Kajabbi.

bull strap: a strong and wide leather belt with a large buckle that is worn loosely around the waist and used to tie the hind legs of a beast that has been thrown.

campdrafting: holding the cattle in a large mob, called a camp, and hence the name. One or two riders on their smartest horses go in and bring the desired beast to the face of the camp, then the nearest ringer turns the cattle back to let the target beast be brought out. That rider then takes it over to the others that have already been camp-drafted out and are held about 100 metres away by two or three ringers. In the case of Augustus, it was drafting out the steers to be taken back to the station steer paddock.

cleanskin: any unbranded and unearmarked cattle, regardless of age.

dinner hobbles: a leather strap with two metal joiners and a buckle. This allows it to be configured as a figure 8 with a hoof going into each of holes. It can be worn as a belt or around the neck of a horse and applied as a precaution in case a horse tethered by the reins pulls away and leaves the rider enjoying lunch riderless. Hence the name, dinner hobbles.

dinner horse: a horse selected to be ridden in the afternoon and usually one that can be caught out in the open and mounted safely without the need of a yard.

earmark: the removal of part of the ear for easy identification of ownership because brands are often very hard to distinguish when hair grows over them. Each station has its own registered earmark and legally it must be applied with cutting pliers specially manufactured for the purpose. The earmark is registered to that property, but is not a legal form of identification.

gilgae: small depressions found in the black-soil downs. They are created over many thousands of years by the uneven ground cracking in the dry season and the cracks filling with broken plant material. Eventually the entire depression becomes a sealed container that gets bigger and is interlinked with others. They fill with water in the wet season. Floating water plants such as Nardoo leave their seeds to bloom again next wet season.

greenhide rope: plaited rope made from untanned hide. Some hair is usually scraped off prior to plaiting.

heifer: a young female from a calf to about two years of age.

mickey: a young bull calf that can be up to a year old and is still a cleanskin so will be castrated.

morning horse: one that is difficult to catch in the open and is better saddled, mounted or ridden in the confines of the yard. Hence it is ridden in the morning.

piker bullock: a very large bullock that has been missed for many years. Without the bone density and effect of testosterone, bullocks tend to keep on growing.

quartpot: a small, oval-shaped billycan with a lid used as a cup and carried in a leather container on the saddle.

spayed cow: a female that has had her ovaries removed and is then fattened for sale along with the bullocks.

stag: a male that was castrated late but retains the characteristics of a bull.

station: can refer to the entire property or to the main buildings and quarters, the difference depending on context; for example, 'We took the steers into the station and got fresh horses' or 'The station has a boundary to the north with Gregory'.

steer: a castrated male up to two or three years of age when it is then regarded as a bullock.

swag: a sheet of canvas about 2 metres long and 1.2 metres wide. Approximately 50 centimetres of its length is folded over and hand sewn to create a pocket to contain clothes and toiletries such as toothbrush and shaving razor. This also creates a pillow. A couple of blankets but no mattresses of any kind create the 'cigarette-thin' swags to pile on the camp truck or fit across the packs on either side of the packhorse.

tail: the riders pushing cattle along from the rear.

weaning: separating young cattle from their mothers. There was no weaning at Augustus in my time and campdrafting was used to pick up the older steers still running in the herd. Some were still running with their mothers, which often prevented them going into calf again.

wing: the riders along the side of the mob determining the direction.

BIBLIOGRAPHY

Australian Dictionary of Biography, various years, Australian National University, Canberra.

Breckwoldt, Roland, 1988, *A Very Elegant Animal: The dingo*, Angus & Robertson, Sydney.

Dalton, Brian James, 1996, 'The Death of John Gilbert', *Lectures on North Queensland History*, James Cook University, Townsville, pp. 22–35.

de Satgé, Oscar, 1901, *Pages from the Journal of a Queensland Squatter*, Hurst and Blackett, London.

Durack, Mary, 1983, *Kings in Grass Castles*, Corgi, Condell Park, p. 127.

Long, S., 2005, *Gidyea Fire: A study of the transformation and maintenance of Aboriginal place properties on the Georgina River*, doctoral thesis, Aboriginal Environments Research Centre, School of Geography, Planning and Architecture, University of Queensland, Brisbane.

May, Dawn, 1994, *Aboriginal Labour and the Cattle Industry: Queensland from white settlement to the present*, Cambridge University Press, Melbourne.

Medical Journal of Australia, 1962, 'The Burketown Epidemic of 1865–1866', vol. 2, issue 8, p. 329.

Powell, J.M., 1991, *Plains of Promise, Rivers of Destiny: Water management and the development of Queensland 1824–1990*, Boolarong Publications, Bowen Hills.

Rebanks, J., 2015, *A Shepherd's Life: A tale of the Lake District*, Penguin Random House, United Kingdom.

Roberts, T., 2005, *Frontier Justice: A history of the Gulf Country to 1900*, University of Queensland Press, Brisbane.